INSTANT POT Cookbook For Beginners

By Rachael Collier

Contents

POULTRY 9
Grandma's Chicken Soup..................................10
Aromatic Creamy Chicken Drumsticks......................11
Tuesday's Chicken Wings with Tzatziki Sauce.............12
Roasted Chicken Breasts with Herbs......................13
Favorite Chicken Wraps..................................14
Wonderful Turkey Legs...................................15
Gourmet Chicken Breasts with Mushrooms..................16
Lazy Cheesy Chicken Casserole...........................17
Sophisticated Chicken Liver.............................18
Perfect Chicken Meatballs...............................19
Basic Chicken Thighs....................................20

PORK 21
Attractive Pork Ribs....................................22
Easy Pulled Pork..23
Italian Sausages with Peppers...........................24
Saturday Pork Chops with Mushroom Sauce.................25
Super-Easy Meatloaf.....................................26
Warm Pork Soup..27
Amazing Pork Cutlets with Mustard Sauce.................28
Most-Liked Pork Salad...................................29
Fragrant Pork Stew......................................30
Papa's Pork Chops with Blue Cheese Sauce................31
Five-Star Ground Pork...................................32

BEEF 33
Instant Ground Beef with Cabbage........................34
Awesome Sausage with Peppers............................35
Monday Meatballs with Parmesan..........................36
Marvellous Beef Steak with Mushroom Sauce...............37
Non-Traditional Beef Bowl...............................38
Sunday's Beef Ribs with Avocado Cream...................39
Colorful Beef Soup......................................40
Light Beef Salad..41
Low-Carb Lasagna with Beef..............................42
Incredible Stuffed Red Peppers with Beef................43
Chili Beef Chuck Roast..................................44

FISH & SEAFOOD 45
King Crabs with Wine Sauce..............................46
Mom's CodFish with Herbs................................47
Tuna Fillets with Arugula...............................48
Tender Salmon with Mayo Sauce...........................49
Piquant Halibut Steaks with Tomato Sauce................50
Red Shrimps with Feta Cheese............................51
Sole Fillets with Steamed Asparagus.....................52
Special Scallops with Sour Cream........................53
Nutritious Seafood Bowl.................................54
Sicilian Fish Soup......................................55
Sardines with Lemon Sauce...............................56

VEGETABLES & SIDE DISHES 57
Friday's Cauliflower Soup...............................58
Greenish Brussels Sprouts with Bacon....................59
Irresistible Kale with Cheese...........................60
Family Tomato Soup......................................61
Zucchini with Mayo-Lemon Dressing.......................62
Tempting Spinach with Cheese............................63

New Asparagus with Cheddar Cheese.......................64
Fast Porcini Mushrooms with Gouda.......................65
Red Stuffed Peppers.....................................66
Creamy Mushroom Soup....................................67
Spectacular Fennel with Goat Cheese.....................68

FAST SNACKS & APPETIZERS 69
Party Turkey Skewers....................................70
Surprising Carrot Meatballs.............................71
Quick Baby Carrots......................................72
Spring Prawn Skewers....................................73
Spicy Pork Bites..74
Spring Deviled Eggs with Bacon..........................75
Yummy Cheese Dip..76
Cocktail Meatballs......................................77
Healthy Asparagus.......................................78
Stuffed Mushrooms with Pancetta and Cheddar.............79
Cauliflower Medley with Ham.............................80
Non-Traditional Eggplant and Ground Beef Bowl 81

EGGS & DAIRY 82
Excellent Spinach Frittata..............................83
Fluffy Eggs with Bacon..................................84
Egg Muffins with Ham....................................85
Rich Casserole with Cheddar Cheese......................86
Stuffed Avocado Boats...................................87
Elementary Deviled Eggs.................................88
Delicious Cheese Soup...................................89
Four-Cheese Dip...90
Fancy Mini Frittatas....................................91
Simple Eggs with Mortadella.............................92
Classic Eggs with Tomato Sauce..........................93
Afternoon Lettuce Sandwiches............................94

VEGAN 95
Marvelous Portobello Mushrooms..........................96
Green Spinach Stew......................................97
Peppery Broccoli..98
Marinated Vegan Cauliflower.............................99
Zucchini with Barbecue Sauce...........................100
The Best Italian Peppers...............................101
Powerful Green Beans with Zucchini.....................102
Vegan Broccoli Soup....................................103
Silk Mushroom Purée....................................104
New Broccoli Balls with Hemp...........................105

DESSERTS 106
Great Strawberry Curd..................................107
Light Cacao Pudding....................................108
Mixed Berries Cobbler..................................109
Fabulous Coconut and Pistachio Crème...................110
Popular Raspberry Porridge.............................111
Tea Almond Cookies.....................................112
Espresso Souffle.......................................113
Old-Fashioned Carrot Cake..............................114
Summer Strawberry Yogurt...............................115
Blueberry Mini Cheesecakes.............................116
Yummy Keto Flan..117

Ketogenic Diet?

A KETO DIET is known as a low carbohydrate and high-fat diet, which allows the body to produce "ketones" and uses them as the main source of energy.

The correct ketone fat-burning diet is represented by a specific ratio of protein, fat, and carbohydrates. Your macronutrient ratio should vary into the following ranges: 50% of calories from fat, 40-45% of calories from protein and 5-10% of calories from carbohydrates.

The goal of a ketogenic diet is to put your body in a metabolic state called ketosis.

Ketosis is a natural process where the body relies on fat as a source of energy. During ketosis, you will be able to lose weight to improve your mental performance and lower the inflammation. As a bonus, ketosis suppresses the appetite and will keep the blood sugar stable.

Why start the Ketogenic Diet?

Weight Loss - During the Keto diet, you can lose weight easily, only eat your healthy fats and proteins. Don't forget to drink plenty of water.

Increase HDL (good cholesterol) - Consuming high amounts of fats during your Ketogenic diet, will decrease the risk of heart disease and increase the levels of HDL (good cholesterol).

Mental Focus - By reducing your carbohydrate intake, you avoid large spikes in blood sugar. This can improve your concentration and focus. Studies have shown that increased fatty acid intake can affect our brain functions.

Blood Pressure - During Ketogenic diet high levels of triglyceride are controlled, therefore you will be saved from many cardiovascular diseases.

Increased energy - You will feel more energized throughout the day, by giving your body a better and more reliable energy source.

Skin Problems - In the blood, during the Keto diet there is minimal production of toxins, hence your skin will be glowing and acne-free.

Research has shown that a keto diet helps obese individuals with insulin resistance to improve insulin sensitivity and restore normal metabolism. Also, the Keto diet is extremely effective for many neurological diseases and conditions such as epilepsy, migraine, Parkinson's, Alzheimer's and even brain tumors.

What foods we should eat on a Keto diet?

Meat and seafood: Snoek, Hake, Salmon, Calamari, Angelfish, Scallops, Trout, Tuna, Sardines, Yellowtail, Prawns, Scallops, Anchovies and Kob, all sausages, Turkey, Chicken, Offal, Pork, Bacon, Lamb, Beef and Duck.

Sweeteners: Stevia, Erythritol, and Xylitol.

Oil and Fats: Coconut milk, Lard, Duck fat, Mayonnaise, Coconut oil, Animal fats, Butter, Macadamia, Avocado oil, Coconut cream, Heavy cream, and Extra virgin olive oil.

Herbs and spices: Granules and Bouillon cubes.

Nuts and Seeds: Macadamia, Walnuts, Hazelnuts, Pecans, Brazils and Almonds, Pumpkin seeds, Sunflower seeds, Chia seeds, Sesame Seeds, and Flax seeds.

Lunch & Deli Meats: Salami, Prosciutto, Ham, Chorizo, Speck, Pastarmi, Bacon, Pepperoncino, Soppressata and Pancetta.

Sauces and Condime: Tomato sauce, Hot sauce, Mustard, Vinegar and Mayonnaise.

Drinks: Tea, Sparkling water, Water and Coffee.

Dairy: Feta cheese, Parmesan cheese, Cream, Butter, Greek yogurt, Cream cheese, Blue cheese, and other high fat cheese.

Flour: Hazelnut flour, Almond flour, Coconut flour, and other nut flours.

Veggies: Kale, Cauliflower, Onions, Radishes Asparagus, Broccoli, Mushrooms, Cabbage, Aubergine, Brussel sprouts, Cucumber, Peppers, Artichokes, Pumpkin, Olives, Spinach, Green beans, and Lettuce.

Fruits: Lemon, Raspberries, Lime, Coconut, Cranberries, Blackberries and Tomato.

Canned food: Sardines, Olives, Sauerkraut, Crab, Pickles, Tuna, Salmon, Anchovies, Tomato (check the nutrition facts label).

Eggs: Organic eggs.

Top 6 Keto Diet Tips

I am sharing with you my top tips to get into and maintain ketosis;

More sleeping - when sleeping more hours, you will easily burn fat.

Use MCT Oil - is good for the gut and support the good bacteria.

Minimize stress - it is easy to get into ketosis when your stress hormones are low.

Always count your carbs - consumption of vegetables will deliver your body all important nutrients

Drink plenty of water - during the Keto diet, your body excretes more water and you should stay hydrated.

Exercise regularly - helps with the balance of your blood sugar and maintain ketosis.

Benefits from your Instant Pot

Nowadays pressure cooking has become very famous. Instant Pot comes to show fresh new ideas by providing healthy and delicious keto meals. The Instant Pot helps food to cook faster by utilizing the power of hot steam. This steam helps force liquid and moisture into the food so dry beans, grains, and tough meats get very tender for a short time.

Now it is time to give you a basic understanding of the cooking functions of your Instant Pot:

SAUTE - Instead of using a pan you can saute food in your Instant Pot. You can use for thickening, simmering, searing or browning.

EGGS - Good setting for cooking eggs. You can select from Less, Normal or More mode, depending on the egg softness or hardness.

SOUP/ BROTH - It is the best program for meaty and veggie soups, broths and creamy chowders.

YOGURT - Make homemade yogurt effortless with this two-step program. For yogurt beginner, you can use 1 tablespoon of prepared yogurt for every quart milk.

BEAN/ CHILI - With this program, you can cook beans for less time. Almost all beans take up to 30 minutes to cook. Use for very soft beans- More mode program, for softer beans- Normal mode and firm texture beans, use the Less mode.

STEAM - This program is good for steaming fish, vegetables and selfish. You should use a steamer basket or metal trivet. If you want to steam vegetables use the Less mode, for fish use the Normal mode and meat- More mode.

RICE - For Basmati rice, cook time is 4-7 minutes, Jasmine rice takes 3-4 minutes, Brown rice takes 22- 27 minutes and Wild rice will require 25-29 minutes. Before pressure cooking, rinse your rise and you should measure a 1:1 ratio of water-to-rice.

SLOW COOK - You can change the cooking time by using the "+/-" button. You can select also the cooking duration (30 minutes to 20 hours) or a cooking mode (Normal, More and Less).

POULTRY- Small portions of chicken will take up to 15 minutes, large pieces of poultry will take 25 minutes and frozen chicken will require around 35 minutes.

MEAT/STEW- This is a good setting for cooking meat. For softer texture use- Less mode and for very tender meat use- More mode.

MULTIGRAIN- This program is good for whole grains, cereal, white rice, and brown rice.

PORRIDGE - It is good for making oatmeal and rice porridge (congee). Use natural pressure release with this function.

NATURAL RELEASE and QUICK RELEASE - There are two ways to release the pressure: Press the "Cancel" button to perform a natural pressure release and quick release- manually release the steam.

MANUAL - This is my favorite setting, you can control very easily the temperature and cooking time.

KEEP WARM / CANCEL - When your Instant Pot completes its cooking cycle, you should press the "Cancel" button. If you don't do that the "Keep Warm" function will be activated automatically to keep food warm.

Top Accessories for Instant Pot

With this accessorize your cooking with instant Pot will be easy and pleasurable.

Steamer Basket - I am using my steamer basket to prepare fish and vegetables. It is a great way to prepare a quick, healthy and delicious meal.

Silicone Lid - over the inner pot, secure the silicon lid and store the leftovers in the fridge.

Extra Sealing Rings - it is good to have different rings for sweet and seafood dishes because flavors transfer very easily.

Casserole Dish - with this dish you can make different keto meals, such as cauliflower casserole, lasagna, etc.

Mason Jars and Ramekins - you need them if you want to make healthy keto desserts and jams.

Gripper Clips - you need this if you don't want to burn your hands while lifting hot food from the Instant pot.

Stackable Steamer Pans - with this accessory is easy to warm leftovers in your Instant pot.

Glass Lid - if you want to see what is cooking inside the pot, you need that.

Extra Inner Cooking Pot - if you often store leftovers in your inner pot, it is good to have a few more extra inner pots.

Egg Steamer Rack - This accessory will prevent eggs from breaking, especially if you like to make hard-boiled eggs.

POULTRY

Grandma's Chicken Soup

Ingredients

- 3 boneless chicken thighs, cut into cubes
- 1 large yellow onion
- 2 tablespoons olive oil
- 1 red bell pepper, seeded and sliced
- 1/2 teaspoon dried basil
- 1 teaspoon dried dill
- 3 cloves garlic, minced
- 1 green bell pepper, seeded and sliced
- 4 cups vegetable broth
- ½ cup Portobello mushrooms, sliced
- Salt and pepper, to taste
- 2 tablespoons fresh parsley, chopped

Nutritional Information

260 Calories
10.5g Fat
5.4g Carbs
37.4g Protein
3.2g Sugars

Directions

Press the "Sauté" button and preheat your Instant Pot. Add the olive oil and sauté the onion and garlic until fragrant.

Add in the mushrooms and peppers. Cook for 3-4 minutes. Then stir in the thighs, vegetable broth, salt, pepper, basil, and dried dill. Combine well.

Secure the lid. Choose "Manual" mode and High pressure. Cook for 6 minutes. When cooking is complete, use a quick pressure release.

Ladle into bowls and sprinkle with fresh parsley. Bon appétit!

Aromatic Creamy Chicken Drumsticks

(Ready in about 15 minutes | Servings 4)

Ingredients

- 1 cup mascarpone cheese
- 4 chicken drumsticks
- ½ teaspoon dried thyme
- Salt and pepper, to taste
- 4 tablespoons pancetta crumbles
- 1 cup of water
- ½ cup cheddar cheese
- ½ teaspoon dried chives

Nutritional Information

453 Calories
31.5g Fat
2g Carbs
38.7g Protein
1.2g Sugars

Directions

Add 1 cup of water to the bottom of the Instant Pot. Then add the mascarpone cheese and chicken drumsticks. Season with salt, pepper, thyme, and chives.

Secure the lid. Choose "Manual" mode and High pressure. Cook for 10 minutes. When cooking is complete, use a quick pressure release.

Stir in the pancetta crumbles and cheddar cheese. Place the lid back on the Instant Pot, press the "Sauté" button and cook for 3 minutes more.

Serve immediately and enjoy!

Tuesday's Chicken Wings with Tzatziki Sauce

(Ready in about 15 minutes | Servings 3)

Ingredients

- 2 lbs. chicken wings
- 1 of cup water
- ½ teaspoon salt
- ½ teaspoon pepper
- ½ teaspoon thyme
- 1 teaspoon marjoram
- 1/2 teaspoon red pepper flakes, crushed
- 2 tablespoons olive oil
- Tzatziki Sauce:
- 2 cups grated cucumber
- 1 cup sour cream
- ½ cup yogurt
- 2 teaspoons dried dill
- 1 ½ tablespoon fresh lemon juice
- 3 cloves garlic, minced
- 1 ½ tablespoon avocado oil

Directions

Add 1 cup of water and a steaming rack into the inner pot. Season the chicken wings with salt, pepper, dried thyme, marjoram, and red pepper flakes.

Secure the lid. Choose "Manual" mode and High pressure and cook for 10 minutes. When cooking is complete, use a quick pressure release.

Meanwhile, mix in a medium bowl all ingredients for the tzatziki sauce. Refrigerate until ready to serve.

Serve the chicken wings with the tzatziki sauce on the side. Bon appétit!

Nutritional Information

425 Calories
18.6g Fat
0.7g Carbs
66.3g Protein
0.4g Sugars

Roasted Chicken Breasts with Herbs

(Ready in about 20 minutes | Servings 4)

Ingredients

- ½ teaspoon onion powder
- 2 tablespoons avocado oil
- 1/2 teaspoon paprika
- 1 teaspoon dried basil
- 4 chicken fillets
- 1/2 teaspoon dried oregano
- 1 cup of water
- ½ teaspoon garlic powder
- 1 teaspoon dried marjoram
- Sea salt, to taste
- 1 cup parmesan cheese, grated

Nutritional Information

506 Calories
20.8g Fat
4.5g Carbs
75.7g Protein
0.1g Sugars

Directions

Massage the chicken fillets with 1 table-spoon of avocado oil and season it with paprika, garlic powder, basil, oregano, marjoram, onion powder, salt, and water.

Press the "Sauté" button and add another tablespoon of avocado oil. Saute the chicken fillets for 2 to 3 minutes per side.

Add 1 cup of water and place the rack into the inner pot. Lower the chicken fillets onto the rack.

Secure the lid. Choose the "Manual" setting and High pressure. Cook for 10 minutes. When cooking is complete, use a natural pressure release and carefully remove the lid.

Serve hot and sprinkle with parmesan. Bon appétit!

Favorite Chicken Wraps

(Ready in about 15 minutes | Servings 7)

Ingredients

- 1 ½ lb. ground chicken
- ½ cup cheddar cheese, shredded
- 1 teaspoon dried oregano
- 1/2 cup vegetable broth
- 1 cup tomato salsa
- 1 yellow onion, chopped
- 1 large-sized head lettuce
- 2 garlic cloves, minced
- 1 green onion, chopped
- ½ green bell pepper, diced
- 1 tablespoon olive oil
- 1/2 teaspoon ground cumin
- Salt and pepper, to taste

Nutritional Information

272 Calories
15.2g Fat
6.9g Carbs
24g Protein
3.1g Sugars

Directions

Press the "Sauté" button and heat the olive oil. Saute the onion and garlic until aromatic.

Add the ground chicken, salt, oregano, pepper, basil, tomato salsa, cumin, and vegetable broth to your Instar Pot.

Secure the lid. Choose the "Manual" setting and High Pressure. Cook for 5 minutes. When cooking is complete, use a natural pressure release and carefully remove the lid.

Divide the chicken mixture among lettuce leaves. Top with cheddar cheese and green bell pepper. Roll up in taco-style. Serve and enjoy!

Wonderful Turkey Legs

Ingredients

- 1 tablespoon fresh rosemary, chopped
- 1 ½ lb. turkey legs
- 2 tablespoons avocado oil
- 1 cup vegetable broth
- 1 tablespoon fresh thyme leaves, chopped
- 1 tablespoon sage leaves
- Salt and pepper, to taste

Nutritional Information

417 Calories
24.5g Fat
1.7g Carbs
44.5g Protein
0.4g Sugars

Directions

Press the "Sauté" button and heat avocado oil. Season the turkey legs with salt and pepper and saute for 3-4 minutes.

Add the vegetable broth, fresh rosemary, fresh thyme leaves, and sage leaves.

Secure the lid. Choose the "Manual" setting and High pressure. Cook for 30 minutes. When cooking is complete, use a natural pressure release and carefully remove the lid.

Serve warm. Bon appetite!

Gourmet Chicken Breasts with Mushrooms

(Ready in about 20 minutes | Servings 3)

Ingredients

- 1 1/2 tablespoon sesame oil
- 1 lb. chicken breast halves, cubed
- 1 yellow onion, chopped
- Salt and pepper, to taste
- 1 cup Cremini mushrooms, thinly sliced
- 1 shallot, chopped
- 2 garlic cloves, minced
- 1 ½ cup chicken broth
- 1/2 cup double cream
- 2 tablespoons fresh parsley, chopped

Nutritional Information

454 Calories
31.7g Fat
6.9g Carbs
33.8g Protein
4.1g Sugars

Directions

Press the "Sauté" button and heat the sesame oil. Saute the garlic and onion until fragrant. Then add the chicken breasts and cook for 4-5 minutes.

Add the mushrooms, shallot, salt, pepper, and chicken broth.

Secure the lid. Choose the "Manual" setting and cook for 9 minutes at High Pressure. When cooking is complete, use a quick pressure release and carefully remove the lid.

Add the double cream and cook until thick. Sprinkle with fresh cilantro and serve. Enjoy!

Lazy Cheesy Chicken Casserole

Ingredients

- 1 1/2 tablespoons sesame oil
- 1 lb. chicken breast halves, cubed
- 1 yellow onion, chopped
- Salt and pepper, to taste
- 1 cup Cremini mushrooms, thinly sliced
- 1 shallot, chopped
- 2 garlic cloves, minced
- 1 ½ cups chicken broth
- 1/2 cup double cream

Nutritional Information

469 Calories
32.3g Fat
8.1g Carbs
36.3g Protein
4.2g Sugars

Directions

Press the "Sauté" button and heat the olive oil. Saute the onion and garlic until aromatic. Add the chicken, basil, salt, pepper, sage, and shallot powder. Cook for 2-3 minutes and stir in the chicken broth.

Secure the lid. Choose the "Meat/Stew" setting and cook for 5 minutes at High pressure. When cooking is complete, use a natural pressure release and carefully remove the lid.

Add the double cream and broccoli and cook until thoroughly heated.

Top with cheddar cheese and serve immediately. Bon appetite!

Sophisticated Chicken Liver

(Ready in about 15 minutes | Servings 3)

Ingredients

- 1 yellow onion, chopped
- 2 tablespoons canola oil
- 1 ½ lb. chicken livers
- 1 teaspoon dried rosemary
- ½ cup red wine
- 1/4 teaspoon dried dill weed
- 1/2 teaspoon paprika
- 3 garlic cloves, crushed
- 1/2 cup of water
- Salt and pepper, to taste

Nutritional Information

381 Calories
20.5g Fat
5.3g Carbs
33.6g Protein
0.3g Sugars

Directions

Press the "Sauté" button and heat the canola oil. Sauté the chicken livers for 2-3 minutes.

Add the yellow onion, dried rosemary, red wine, dried dill, paprika, crushed garlic, water, salt, and pepper to taste.

Secure the lid. Choose the "Manual" setting and cook for 10 minutes at High pressure. When cooking is complete, use a quick pressure release and carefully remove the lid.

Serve warm. Bon appetite!

Perfect Chicken Meatballs

(Ready in about 15 minutes | Servings 3)

Ingredients

- 1 lb. ground chicken
- 2 eggs
- 1 small yellow onion, finely chopped
- 1/3 cup pork rind crumbs
- ½ teaspoon salt
- ½ teaspoon pepper
- 1/3 teaspoon dried marjoram
- 1/2 teaspoon dried oregano
- ½ cup gouda cheese, shredded
- 2 tablespoons parmesan cheese, shredded
- 2 tablespoons sesame oil
- 1 ½ cup tomato sauce
- 1/2 cup of water
- 1 ½ tablespoon fresh parsley, chopped

Nutritional Information

382 Calories
26.4g Fat
3.8g Carbs
32.8g Protein
1.6g Sugars

Directions

In a large bowl mix the yellow onion, ground chicken, egg, pork rind crumbs, salt, pepper, dried oregano, fresh parsley, dried marjoram, gouda cheese, and parmesan. Combine well and shape the mixture into balls.

Press the "Sauté" button and heat the sesame oil. Saute the meatballs for 1-2 minutes and add the tomato sauce and water.

Secure the lid. Choose the "Manual" setting and cook for 7 minutes under High pressure. When cooking is complete, use a quick pressure release and carefully remove the lid.

Serve your meatballs and top with the tomato sauce. Bon appétit!

Basic Chicken Thighs

Ingredients

- 4 chicken thighs
- 2 tablespoons avocado oil
- 1/2 teaspoon dried basil
- 1 teaspoon dried oregano
- 1/2 cup chicken broth
- 1/3 cup white wine
- Salt and pepper, to taste
- 4 garlic cloves, minced
- 1 teaspoon paprika
- 1/2 teaspoon dried marjoram

Nutritional Information

496 Calories
34.1g Fat
4.7g Carbs
32.7g Protein
2.2g Sugars

Directions

Press the "Sauté" button and heat the avocado oil. Saute the chicken thighs for 2-3 minutes.

Then stir in the paprika, white wine, garlic, salt, pepper, dried basil, dried oregano, chicken broth and dried marjoram.

Secure the lid. Choose the "Manual" setting and cook for 13 minutes. When cooking is complete, use a natural pressure release and carefully remove the lid.

Serve with your favorite keto salad. Bon appétit!

PORK

Attractive Pork Ribs

Ingredients

- 2 lbs. spare ribs
- 1 teaspoon salt
- 1 teaspoon pepper
- 1 teaspoon garlic powder
- 1 teaspoon onion powder
- 1 teaspoon smoked paprika
- 1 teaspoon dried oregano
- ½ cup tomato puree
- 2 tablespoons olive oil
- 2 tablespoons fresh lemon juice
- 2 tablespoons sesame oil

Nutritional Information

527 Calories
46.2g Fat
5g Carbs
34.9g Protein
1.9g Sugars

Directions

In a large dish mix the lemon juice, salt, pepper, garlic powder, onion powder, smoked paprika, olive oil, dried oregano, and tomato puree.

Add the spare ribs to the dish and marinate for at least 3 hours.

Remove the spare ribs from the marinade. Then press the "Sauté" button and heat the sesame oil. Add the spare ribs and brown them for 2 minutes per side.

Secure the lid. Choose the "Meat/Stew" setting and cook for 25 minutes under High pressure. When cooking is complete, use a natural pressure release and carefully remove the lid.

Serve warm with your favorite Keto salad. Bon appetite!

Easy Pulled Pork

(Ready in about 45 minutes | Servings 4)

Ingredients

- 2 tablespoons olive oil
- 1 teaspoon onion powder
- 1/2 teaspoon mustard seeds
- ½ teaspoon salt
- 2 lbs. pork roast, cut into cubes
- ½ teaspoon garlic powder
- ½ teaspoon pepper
- 1 tablespoon cumin
- 1/2 teaspoon paprika
- 1 cup vegetable broth

Nutritional Information

511 Calories
27.2g Fat
2.5g Carbs
50.6g Protein
0.8g Sugars

Directions

Season the pork roast with salt and pepper.

Press the "Sauté" button and heat the olive oil. Sear the pork for 2-3 minutes on all sides.

Stir in the onion powder, mustard seeds, cumin, garlic powder, paprika, and vegetable broth.

Secure the lid. Choose the "Manual" setting and cook for 35 minutes under High pressure. When cooking is complete, use a natural pressure release and carefully remove the lid.

Shred the meat with two forks and serve warm. Enjoy!

Italian Sausages with Peppers

Ingredients

- 1 green red bell pepper, sliced
- 2 garlic cloves, minced
- 1 yellow onion, chopped
- 1 red bell pepper, sliced
- 1 ½ cup tomato sauce
- ½ cup vegetable broth
- 1 teaspoon dried basil
- 4 Italian sausage links
- 1/2 teaspoon dried oregano
- 1 yellow red bell pepper, sliced
- 1/2 teaspoon dried rosemary
- 1 cup parmesan cheese, shredded

Directions

Add all listed ingredients (without the parmesan cheese) to your Instant Pot.

Secure the lid. Choose the "Manual" setting and cook for 15 minutes under High pressure. When cooking is complete, use a quick pressure release and carefully remove the lid.

Sprinkle with parmesan and serve immediately. Bon appetite!

Nutritional Information

388 Calories
16.9g Fat
7g Carbs
22.3g Protein
1.2g Sugars

Saturday Pork Chops with Mushroom Sauce

(Ready in about 15 minutes | Servings 5)

Ingredients

- 5 pork chops
- 1/2 cup scallions, chopped
- 1 tablespoon arrowroot powder + 1 tablespoon water
- 2 teaspoons sesame oil
- 1/2 cup heavy cream
- 1 cup Cremini mushrooms, thinly sliced
- 1 cup chicken broth
- 1 ½ Worcestershire sauce
- Salt and pepper, to taste

Nutritional Information

401 Calories
23.8g Fat
2.2g Carbs
41.7g Protein
1.2g Sugars

Directions

Press the "Sauté" button and heat the sesame oil. Season the pork chops with salt and pepper.

Sear the pork chops until lightly brown. Then, stir in the Cremini mushrooms, scallions, and chicken broth to the Instant Pot.

Secure the lid. Choose the "Manual" setting and cook for 9 minutes under High pressure. When cooking is complete, use a quick pressure release and carefully remove the lid. Remove the pork chops from the Instant Pot.

Then, in a small bowl mix the arrowroot powder with water. Then add it to the Instant Pot along with the heavy cream and Worcestershire sauce.

Press the "Sauté" button again and cook until the mixture gets thick. Serve warm and enjoy!

Super-Easy Meatloaf

Ingredients

- 1 cup burrata cheese,
- 1 yellow onion, diced
- 1/3 cup tomato sauce
- 2 tablespoons fresh parsley, chopped
- 1/2 teaspoon pepper
- 1 lb. ground pork
- 1 teaspoon red pepper
- 1 egg, whisked
- 1 carrot, diced
- 4 thin slices Prosciutto Cotto
- 1/2 teaspoon salt

Nutritional Information

502 Calories
38.9g Fat
6g Carbs
35.6g Protein
2.7g Sugars

Directions

Place a metal rack and 1 cup of water to the bottom of your inner pot in the Instant Pot.

In a large bowl mix the ground pork, burrata cheese, salt, pepper, diced onion, carrot, fresh parsley, red pepper, and egg.

Shape the mixture into the meatloaf. Place the meatloaf in a baking pan.

Arrange the prosciutto cotto slices, crosswise over the meatloaf, overlapping them slightly. Top with the tomato sauce.

Secure the lid. Choose the "Manual" setting and cook for 19 minutes at High pressure. When cooking is complete, use a quick pressure release and carefully remove the lid.

Serve warm and enjoy!

Warm Pork Soup

Ingredients

- 1 ½ lb. pork butt, cut into cubes
- 2 tablespoons canola oil
- 1 teaspoon onion powder
- 2 scallions, chopped
- 1 yellow bell pepper, chopped
- 1 cup Kale
- Salt and pepper, to taste
- 6 cups vegetable broth
- 1 carrot, shredded
- 1 teaspoon garlic powder
- 6 lemon wedges

Nutritional Information

388 Calories

29.5g Fat

7g Carbs

2.6g Fiber

25g Protein

3g Sugars

Directions

Preheat your Instant Pot by pressing the "Sauté" button and heat the canola oil. Cook the pork cubes for 2-3 minutes stirring occasionally.

Add in the scallion, yellow bell pepper, onion powder, garlic powder, carrot, vegetable broth, salt, and pepper.

Secure the lid. Choose the "Manual" mode and cook for 5 minutes at High pressure. When cooking is complete, use a quick pressure release and carefully remove the lid.

Stir in the kale and let it simmer for 2 minutes more. Serve hot and garnish with lemon wedges. Bon appetite!

Amazing Pork Cutlets with Mustard Sauce

(Ready in about 20 minutes | Servings 3)

Ingredients

- 2 tablespoons avocado oil
- 1/2 teaspoon salt
- 3 pork cutlets
- 2 tablespoons Dijon mustard
- 1/2 teaspoon paprika
- 1/2 teaspoon garlic powder
- 1/3 cup heavy cream
- ½ teaspoon onion powder
- 2 teaspoons dried rosemary
- ½ cup pork broth
- ½ teaspoon pepper
- 1 tablespoon arrowroot powder + 1 tablespoon water

Nutritional Information

480 Calories
32.4g Fat
2.7g Carbs
40g Protein
0.8g Sugars

Directions

Press the "Sauté" button and heat the avocado oil. Season the pork cutlets with salt and pepper. Sear the cutlets for 1 minute on each side.

Stir in the paprika, garlic powder, dried rosemary, pork broth, and onion powder.

Secure the lid. Choose the "Manual" setting and cook for 8 minutes under High pressure. When cooking is complete, use a quick pressure release and carefully remove the lid. Remove the pork cutlets from the Instant Pot.

In a small bowl mix the arrowroot powder with water. Then add it to the Instant Pot along with the heavy cream and Dijon mustard.

Set the Instant Pot to "Saute" and cook for 2 minutes more. Serve the pork cutlets and top with the mustard sauce. Bon appetite!

Most-Liked Pork Salad

Ingredients

- 1 cup vegetable broth
- 2 shallots chopped
- 1 cup baby spinach, washed and rinsed
- 1 lb. pork tenderloin
- ½ cup blue cheese
- 2 teaspoons olive oil
- 2 teaspoons tamari sauce
- 1 cup arugula
- 1 tablespoon lemon juice
- 1 cup kale
- 1 tablespoon white wine vinegar
- 2 teaspoons sesame seeds

Nutritional Information

352 Calories
16.1g Fat
4.4g Carbs
45.6g Protein
1.8g Sugars

Directions

Season the pork tenderloin with salt and pepper. Then add the steak and vegetable broth to the inner pot.

Secure the lid. Choose the "Meat/Stew" setting and cook for 25 minutes at High pressure. When cooking is complete, use a natural pressure release and carefully remove the lid.

Leave the pork tenderloin to cool completely. Shred the meat and transfer to a salad bowl.

Add the shallots, kale, arugula, baby spinach, and blue cheese.

Now, make the dressing by mixing the olive oil, tamari sauce, white wine vinegar, and lemon juice. Combine well.

Drizzle the dressing over the salad. Sprinkle with sesame seeds and serve. Bon appetite!

Fragrant Pork Stew

Ingredients

- 2 garlic cloves, finely minced
- 1 red bell pepper, sliced
- 1 tablespoon fresh cilantro leaves, chopped
- 2 tablespoons fresh rosemary, chopped
- 1 lb. pork butt
- 2 cups baby carrots
- 1 large yellow onion, chopped
- 2 tablespoons sesame oil
- 1 cup vegetable broth
- 1/2 cup black olives, pitted and sliced
- 1 green bell pepper, sliced
- Salt and pepper, to taste

Nutritional Information

447 Calories
31.6g Fat
7g Carbs
29.8g Protein
3.4g Sugars

Directions

Slice the pork butt into -inch cubes.

Preheat your Instant Pot by pressing the "Sauté" button and heat the sesame oil. Season the pork cubes with salt and pepper.

Sear the pork cubes for 2 minutes per side. Stir in the chopped onion, green bell pepper, garlic, baby carrots, sliced red bell peppers, and vegetable broth.

Season with fresh rosemary and cilantro. Mix well.

Secure the lid. Choose the "Meat/Stew" mode and cook for 20 minutes at High pressure. When cooking is complete, use a quick pressure release and carefully remove the lid.

Serve warm garnished with black olives. Bon appétit!

Papa's Pork Chops with Blue Cheese Sauce

Ingredients

- 3 boneless pork chops
- Salt and pepper, to taste
- 1 shallot, sliced
- 1/3 cup white wine
- 2 tablespoons avocado oil
- 1/2 cup chicken broth
- 1/2 cup blue cheese
- 1/2 cup double cream
- 1 tablespoon scallion, chopped

Nutritional Information

490 Calories
30.1g Fat;4.1g Carbs
49.8g Protein
3g Sugars

Directions

Press the "Sauté" button and heat the avocado oil. Sear the pork chops for 2 minutes per side and set aside.

If necessary, clean the brown bits from the Instant pot with wooden spoon.

Add the shallot, white wine and chicken broth. Mix well.

Place the pork chops back in the Instant Pot. Secure the lid. Choose the "Manual" mode and cook for 9 minutes at High pressure. When cooking is complete, use a natural pressure release and carefully remove the lid.

Seal the lid and stir in the double cream and blue cheese, serve the pork chops warm and sprinkle with fresh scallion. Bon appetite!

Five- Star Ground Pork

Ingredients

- 1 ½ lb. ground pork
- 1 red onion, chopped
- 1 can diced tomatoes
- 1 teaspoon dried basil
- 3 cloves garlic, peeled
- 1 red bell pepper, chopped
- 1 teaspoon dried oregano
- 1/3 cup red wine
- 2 tablespoons sesame oil
- 1 cup vegetable broth
- 2 tablespoons fresh basil leaves, snipped
- ½ teaspoon pepper
- 1/2 teaspoon dried dill weed
- 1 bay leaf
- ½ teaspoon salt

Nutritional Information

517 Calories
35.8g Fat
7g Carbs
30.5g Protein
3g Sugars

Directions

Press the "Sauté" button and preheat your Instant Pot. Add the sesame oil and sauté the ground pork until browned.

Stir in the onion, garlic and bell pepper. Cook until aromatic. Then add diced tomatoes, bay leaf, dried dill, salt, pepper, dried oregano, dried basil, vegetable broth, and red wine.

Secure the lid. Choose the "Manual" setting and cook for 9 minutes at High pressure. When cooking is complete, use a quick pressure release and carefully remove the lid.

Serve into bowls and garnish with fresh basil leaves. Bon appétit!

BEEF

Instant Ground Beef with Cabbage

Ingredients

- 2 tablespoons olive oil
- 1 ½ lb. ground beef
- ½ teaspoon pepper
- 1 cup beef broth
- 4 cups green cabbage, chopped
- 1 tablespoon soy sauce
- 1 teaspoon dried marjoram
- 2 garlic cloves, pressed
- 1 can tomato puree
- ½ teaspoon salt
- 1 large yellow onion, diced
- 1 teaspoon dried thyme

Nutritional Information

491 Calories
28.7g Fat
7g Carbs
38.5g Protein
1.8g Sugars

Directions

Press the "Sauté" button and heat the olive oil. Saute the onion and garlic until aromatic.

Stir in the ground beef and cook until brown. Then add the tomato pure, beef broth, green cabbage, soy sauce, dried marjoram, dried thyme, salt, and pepper.

Secure the lid. Choose "Manual" mode and High pressure; cook for 20 minutes. When cooking is complete, use a natural pressure release and carefully remove the lid.

Serve warm. Bon appétit!

Awesome Sausage with Peppers

Ingredients

- 2 cloves garlic, minced
- 1 cup vegetable broth
- 2 red bell peppers, sliced
- 4 beef sausages, casing removed and sliced
- Salt and pepper, to taste
- 1/2 teaspoon paprika
- 2 yellow bell peppers, sliced
- 1 teaspoon dried rosemary
- 1 yellow onion, diced
- 2 bay leaves
- 2 fresh Roma tomatoes, puréed
- 1 jalapeño pepper, chopped
- 2 tablespoons sesame oil

Nutritional Information

290 Calories
14.7g Fat
7g Carbs
12.5g Protein
2.6g Sugars

Directions

Press the "Sauté" button and heat the sesame oil. Sear the sausages for 3 minutes, stirring periodically. Set aside.

Then, add the onion and garlic and cook until translucent. Stir in the red bell peppers, vegetable broth, paprika, yellow bell peppers, dried rosemary, bay leaves, pureed Roma tomatoes, salt, pepper, and reserved sausage.

Secure the lid. Choose "Manual" mode and High pressure; cook for 18 minutes. When cooking is complete, use a quick pressure release and carefully remove the lid.

Sprinkle with chopped jalapeno pepper and serve immediately. Bon appétit!

Monday Meatballs with Parmesan

Ready in about 30 minutes | Servings 5)

Ingredients

- 1 yellow onion, diced
- 2 cloves garlic, minced
- 2 small eggs, beaten
- ½ cup pork rinds
- 1/3 cup parmesan cheese
- Salt and pepper, to taste
- 2 tablespoons canola oil
- 1 lb. ground beef
- 1 ½ can tomato puree
- 1 cup vegetable broth
- 2 teaspoons dried basil

Nutritional Information

401 Calories
19.8g Fat
7g Carbs
33.5g Protein
3.6g Sugars

Directions

In a large bowl mix the ground beef, eggs, garlic, yellow onion, pork rinds, parmesan, salt and pepper.

Shape the mixture into 1-inch meatballs. Then press the "Sauté" button and heat the canola oil. Saute the meatballs for 5-6 minutes.

Pour the tomato puree, basil, vegetable broth and crushed tomatoes over the meatballs.

Secure the lid. Choose the "Manual" mode and cook for 12 minutes at High pressure. When cooking is complete, use a natural pressure release for 10 minutes and carefully remove the lid.

Serve warm. Bon appétit!

Marvellous Beef Steak with Mushroom Sauce

(Ready in about 30 minutes | Servings 3)

Ingredients

- 1 lb. beef top sirloin steak
- 1 cup vegetable broth
- ½ teaspoon dried thyme
- 1 tablespoon olive oil
- 2 garlic cloves, minced
- Salt and pepper, to taste
- ½ teaspoon dried sage
- For the Sauce:
- 1 1/2 cup Shiitake mushrooms, sliced
- 1/2 cup sour cream
- 1 tablespoon butter, softened
- ½ cup Swiss cheese, shredded

Nutritional Information

392 Calories
26.9g Fat
5.4g Carbs
30.4g Protein
1.4g Sugars

Directions

Press the "Sauté" button to heat the olive oil. Sear the steak for 2-3 minutes or until brown.

Stir in the garlic, salt, sage, pepper, thyme, and vegetable broth.

Secure the lid. Choose "Manual" mode and High pressure; cook for 15 minutes. When cooking is complete, use a quick pressure release and carefully remove the lid.

Take the meat out of the Instant Pot. Leave to cool and then, slice it into strips.

Press the "Sauté" button again and melt the butter. Add the mushrooms to the Instant Pot and cook for 4 minutes.

Add the sour cream and Swiss cheese. Simmer for a couple of minutes. Then, return the meat to the Instant Pot and serve. Enjoy!

Non-Traditional Beef Bowl

Ingredients

- 1 yellow onion chopped
- 1 teaspoon chili powder
- 2 teaspoons smoked paprika
- ½ teaspoon dried cumin
- ½ teaspoon dried oregano
- 1 cup vegetable broth
- 1 red bell pepper, deseeded and sliced
- 1 can diced tomatoes
- 1 lb. ground beef
- 1 cup cheddar cheese, shredded
- 1 tablespoon olive oil
- Salt and pepper, to taste
- 1 tablespoon soy sauce
- 1/3 cup fresh cilantro leaves, chopped

Nutritional Information

344 Calories
19.6g Fat
7g Carbs
33.4g Protein
3.4g Sugars

Directions

Press the "Sauté" button to preheat your Instant Pot. Heat the olive oil and cook the ground beef for 3 minutes.

Then stir in the red bell pepper, vegetable broth, onion, tomatoes, soy sauce. chili powder, smoked paprika, salt, pepper, cumin, and oregano.

Secure the lid. Choose the "Manual" mode and cook for 8 minutes at High pressure. When cooking is complete, use a natural pressure release and carefully remove the lid.

Serve into bowls and top with the shredded cheddar cheese and fresh cilantro. Bon appetite!

Sunday's Beef Ribs
with Avocado Cream

(Ready in about 25 minutes | Servings 6)

Ingredients

- 1 ½ tablespoon avocado oil
- 2 lbs. beef short ribs
- 1/2 teaspoon red pepper
- 1 teaspoon salt
- 1teaspoon pepper
- Avocado Cream:
- 1/3 cup yogurt
- 1/2 cup sour cream
- 1 teaspoon garlic powder
- 1 tablespoon fresh lime juice
- 1 large avocado, pitted and halved

Nutritional Information

421 Calories

29.4g Fat

6.9g Carbs

33.4g Protein

1.5g Sugars

Directions

- Press the "Sauté" button and preheat the Instant Pot. Then, heat the avocado oil. Sear the ribs until brown on all sides. Season the ribs with red pepper, salt, and pepper.
- Secure the lid. Choose "Manual" mode and High pressure; cook for 18 minutes. When cooking is complete, use a quick pressure release and carefully remove the lid.
- Meanwhile, in a small bowl combine the avocado, sour cream, yogurt, garlic powder, and fresh lime juice. Place in the refrigerator until ready to serve.
- Serve the ribs warm and top with the avocado cream. Enjoy!

Colorful Beef Soup

(Ready in about 30 minutes | Servings 4)

Ingredients

- 2 tablespoons vegetable oil
- 1 lb. beef chuck, cut into cubes
- Salt and pepper, to taste
- 4 cups beef broth
- 2 teaspoons dried oregano
- 1 carrot, diced
- 4 cloves garlic, sliced
- 1 cup Cremini mushrooms, sliced
- 1 ½ cup zucchini, spiralized
- 1 large red bell pepper, chopped
- 2 scallions, chopped

Nutritional Information

253 Calories
13.4g Fat
6.7g Carbs
24.3g Protein
2.5g Sugars

Directions

Press the "Sauté" button to preheat your Instant Pot. Heat the vegetable oil and add the beef cubes. Cook for 2-3 minutes.

Then add the scallions, carrot, and garlic. Saute for 1 minute. Stir in the beef broth, dried oregano, red bell pepper, spiralized zucchini, mushrooms, salt, and pepper.

Secure the lid. Choose the "Manual" mode and cook for 10 minutes at High pressure. When cooking is complete, use a quick pressure release for 10 minutes and carefully remove the lid.

Serve warm. Bon appetite!

Light Beef Salad

(Ready in about 30 minutes | Servings 5)

Ingredients

- 1 cup vegetable broth
- 1 lb. sirloin steak, cut into small cubes
- 1/2 cup green onions, chopped
- 1 ½ cucumber, thinly sliced
- 1 ½ cup red cabbage, sliced
- 2 tablespoons fresh cilantro, chopped
- 1 ½ cup bok choy cabbage, sliced
- 2 teaspoons sesame seeds
- 2 tablespoons fresh lemon juice
- 2 tablespoon canola oil
- 2 tablespoons extra-virgin olive oil

Nutritional Information

236 Calories
11.6g Fat
4.3g Carbs
29.4g Protein
1.9g Sugars

Directions

Press the "Sauté" button to preheat your Instant Pot. Heat the canola oil and add the beef cubes. Cook for 2 minutes and stir in the vegetable broth.

Secure the lid. Choose "Meat/Stew" mode and High pressure; cook for 20 minutes. When cooking is complete, use a natural pressure release and carefully remove the lid.

Leave the beef to cool and transfer to a large salad bowl.

Then, add the cucumber, green onion, red cabbage, bok choy cabbage, sesame seeds, and fresh cilantro. Drizzle the salad with lemon juice and olive oil.

Mix well and serve. Bon appétit!

Low-Carb Lasagna with Beef

Ingredients

- ½ teaspoon oregano
- 1 large zucchini, cut into thin slices
- 1 cup bacon, chopped
- 3 tablespoons yellow onion, chopped
- 2 eggs
- 2 cups tomato puree
- 1/2 cup double cream
- 1 lb. ground pork
- 1 teaspoon dried basil
- 1/2 cup heavy cream
- Salt and pepper, to taste
- 2 tablespoons olive oil
- 1 ½ cup mozzarella cheese
- ½ teaspoon marjoram

Nutritional Information

481 Calories
28.7g Fat
7g Carbs
39.2g Protein
2.6g Sugars

Directions

Press the "Sauté" button and heat the olive oil. Cook the ground pork for 3 minutes.

Then add the onion and garlic, saute until aromatic

In a large bowl combine the eggs, puréed tomatoes, heavy cream, double cream, salt, pepper, marjoram, basil, oregano, and ½ cup mozzarella cheese.

In a casserole dish, place a layer of the ground meat. Then, create 2 layers of the zucchini crisscrossing.

Add a layer of the cheese/cream mixture and top with 1 cup mozzarella cheese.

Secure the lid. Choose "Meat/Stew" mode and High pressure; cook for 30 minutes. When cooking is complete, use a quick pressure release and carefully remove the lid.

Leave to cool and slice. Serve and enjoy!

Incredible Stuffed Red Peppers with Beef

Ingredients

- 4 large red bell peppers, washed, deseeded and cored
- 1 yellow onion, chopped
- 2 garlic cloves, minced
- 1/2 cup bacon, chopped
- 1/2 carrot, finely chopped
- Salt and pepper, to taste
- 2 teaspoons marjoram
- 1 teaspoon basil
- 2 tablespoons fresh parsley, chopped
- 1 ½ cup tomato puree
- 1 lb. ground beef
- 1 cup cheddar cheese, grated
- 1 cup of water

Nutritional Information

306 Calories
11.5g Fat
6.9g Carbs
27.6g Protein
3.4g Sugars

Directions

In a large bowl mix the ground beef, onion, green onion, bacon, parsley, carrot, basil, marjoram, tomato puree, garlic, salt, and pepper.

Add 1 cup of water and a metal trivet to the bottom. Fill the pepper with the mixture

Lower the casserole dish onto the trivet in the Instant Pot.

Secure the lid. Choose the "Manual" mode and cook for 13 minutes at High pressure. When cooking is complete, use a natural pressure release for 10 minutes and carefully remove the lid.

Then top the peppers with the grated cheddar cheese, close the lid and set to "Warm" for 3-4 minutes.

Serve immediately and enjoy!

Chili Beef Chuck Roast

(Ready in about 20 minutes | Servings 3)

Ingredients

- 1 lb. blade chuck roast
- 1/3 cup fresh chives, chopped
- 1 large Romano tomato, puréed
- ½ teaspoon salt
- 2 tablespoons fresh coriander, chopped
- ½ teaspoon onion powder
- 1/2 teaspoon red pepper flakes, crushed
- ½ teaspoon garlic powder
- 1 tablespoon sesame oil
- ½ teaspoon pepper
- 1 jalapeño pepper, seeded and diced
- 1 teaspoon chili powder
- 1 cup of water

Nutritional Information

296 Calories
15.2g Fat
6.1g Carbs
33.7g Protein
2.8g Sugars

Directions

Press the "Sauté" button and preheat your Instant Pot. Add the sesame oil and cook the beef for 2-3 minutes per side.

Stir in the tomato, salt, coriander, pepper, onion powder, red pepper flakes, garlic powder, chili powder, water, and jalapeño pepper. Combine well.

Secure the lid. Choose "Manual" mode and High pressure; cook for 13 minutes. When cooking is complete, use a natural pressure release and carefully remove the lid.

Shred the chuck roast with a fork and serve. Top with fresh chives. Bon appétit!

FISH & SEAFOOD

King Crabs with Wine Sauce

Ingredients

- 3 lbs. frozen king crab legs
- 1/2 cup water
- 1/3 cup lemon juice
- 1/3 cup dry white wine
- Sea salt and pepper, to taste
- 1 tablespoon sesame oil
- 1/2 tablespoon fresh thyme, chopped

Nutritional Information

351 Calories
8.9g Fat
2.7g Carbs
64.4g Protein
1.3g Sugars

Directions

Add the frozen king crab legs, sesame oil, water, dry white wine, fresh thyme, salt, and pepper to the inner pot.

Secure the lid. Choose the "Manual" mode and cook for 3 minutes at High pressure. When cooking is complete, use a quick pressure release and carefully remove the lid.

Serve the crab legs warm and drizzle with the lemon juice Enjoy!

Mom's CodFish with Herbs

(Ready in about 10 minutes | Servings 4)

Ingredients

- 1/2 cup hot water
- 2 tablespoons olive oil
- Sea salt and pepper, to taste
- 1/3 teaspoon paprika
- 1 tablespoon oregano, chopped
- 4 fresh codfish fillets
- 1 tablespoon fresh basil, chopped
- ½ teaspoon onion powder
- ½ teaspoon garlic powder
- 4 lemon slices
- 2 tablespoons fresh parsley, chopped

Nutritional Information

276 Calories
8.9g Fat
5.2g Carbs
44.1g Protein
2g Sugars

Directions

Add the hot water into the inner pot and put the steamer rack.

Place the codfish fillets on the rack. Season the fillets with fresh oregano, olive oil, fresh basil, onion powder, paprika, garlic powder, salt, pepper, and fresh parsley.

Secure the lid. Choose the "Steam" mode and cook for 3 minutes at Low pressure. When cooking is complete, use a quick pressure release and carefully remove the lid.

Remove the codfish fillets from the inner pot and transfer them into plates.

Top with fresh parsley and lemon slices. Serve! Bon appetite!

Tuna Fillets with Arugula

Ingredients

- 2 lbs. tuna filets
- 2 ½ cup arugula
- 1 cup of water
- 2 tablespoons ghee
- Salt and pepper, to taste
- ½ cup fresh lemon juice

Nutritional Information

210 Calories

7.9g Fat

2.6g Carbs

44.6g Protein

1.8g Sugars

Directions

Put the water in the inner pot and place the steamer rack.

Place the tuna fillets onto the rack. Brush the tuna fillets with ghee and season with salt and pepper.

Secure the lid. Choose the "Steam" mode and cook for 4 minutes at Low pressure. When cooking is complete, use a quick pressure release and carefully remove the lid.

Serve warm with the arugula and drizzle with fresh lemon juice. Bon appetite!

Tender Salmon with Mayo Sauce

Ingredients

- 1/2 teaspoon garlic powder
- 1 lb. salmon fillets
- 1 tablespoon olive oil
- 1/2 lemon, cut into wedges
- 1 cup of water
- ½ teaspoon thyme
- ½ teaspoon rosemary
- Sea salt and pepper, to taste
- Mayo sauce:
- ½ cup mayonnaise
- ½ teaspoon garlic powder
- 1 tablespoon fresh dill, chopped
- 1/3 cup yogurt

Nutritional Information

401 Calories
25.6g Fat
5.6g Carbs
33.8g Protein
2.5g Sugars

Directions

Place 1 cup of water and a metal rack to the inner pot of the Instant Pot.

Place the salmon fillets on the rack. Season the fillets with garlic powder, salt, pepper, thyme, and rosemary.

Secure the lid. Choose the "Steam" mode and cook for 3 minutes at Low pressure. When cooking is complete, use a quick pressure release and carefully remove the lid.

Meanwhile, in a medium bowl mix the mayonnaise, yogurt, fresh dill, and garlic powder. Combine well.

Serve the fish warm and top with the mayo sauce and lemon wedges. Bon appetite!

Piquant Halibut Steaks with Tomato Sauce

(Ready in about 15 minutes | Servings 4)

Ingredients

- 1/2 teaspoon red pepper flakes, crushed
- 1 lb. halibut steaks
- 2 tablespoons olive oil
- 2 tablespoons fresh lemon juice
- Sea salt and pepper, to taste
- 1 cup of water
- 1 tablespoon olive oil
- 1 red bell pepper, sliced
- 1 yellow onion, diced
- 1 can diced tomatoes
- 1 teaspoon turmeric powder
- 1/3 cup vegetable broth
- 1 jalapeno pepper, diced
- 1 teaspoon dried basil

Nutritional Information

324 Calories
25.8g Fat
5.3g Carbs
18.7g Protein
2.9g Sugars

Directions

Add 1 cup of water and a steamer rack to the bottom of your Instant Pot.

Cut 4 sheets of aluminum foil. Place the halibut steak in each sheet of foil. Add the olive oil, salt, and black pepper to the top of the fish and close each packet and seal the edges.

Lower the packets onto the rack.

Secure the lid. Choose the "Steam" mode and cook for 3 minutes at Low pressure. When cooking is complete, use a natural pressure release and carefully remove the lid. Reserve.

Then, add the olive oil, yellow onion, diced tomatoes, turmeric, vegetable broth, jalapeno pepper, dried basil, red bell pepper, and red pepper flakes.

Secure the lid. Choose the "Steam" mode and cook for 4 minutes at Low pressure. When cooking is complete, use a quick pressure release and carefully remove the lid.

Serve the halibut steaks and top with the tomato sauce. Bon appetite!

Red Shrimps with Feta Cheese

(Ready in about 10 minutes | Servings 4)

Ingredients

- 1 ½ can diced tomatoes
- 1 teaspoon basil
- 1 large onion, chopped
- 2 tablespoons canola oil
- 1 1/2 lb. raw shrimp, shelled and deveined
- 3 cloves garlic, diced
- 1 teaspoon turmeric
- 1 cup Asiago cheese, shredded
- ½ cup vegetable stock
- 1/2 teaspoon dried oregano

Directions

Add the garlic, onion, canned tomatoes, shrimps, canola oil, basil, vegetable stock, turmeric, oregano, and tomatoes to the inner pot.

Secure the lid. Choose the "Manual" mode and cook for 3 minutes at Low pressure. When cooking is complete, use a quick pressure release and carefully remove the lid.

Top with Asiago cheese and serve.

Nutritional Information

392 Calories
19.8g Fat
6.1g Carbs
44.6g Protein
2.8g Sugars

Sole Fillets with Steamed Asparagus

Ingredients

- 2 tablespoons fresh parsley
- 3 cloves garlic, minced
- 3 cups fresh asparagus, trimmed
- 1 teaspoon dried rosemary
- 2 small shallots, quartered
- 2 tablespoons butter
- 1 1/2 lb. sole fillet
- ½ teaspoon dried thyme
- ½ cup vegetable broth
- 1 lemon, cut into wedges
- Sea salt and pepper, to taste

Nutritional Information

279 Calories

10.4g Fat

6g Carbs

40.69g Protein

3.2g Sugars

Directions

Season the sole fillets with salt and pepper. Place the sole fillets to the inner pot and secure the lid.

Choose the "Steam" mode and cook for 3 minutes at Low pressure. When cooking is complete, use a quick pressure release and carefully remove the lid. Reserve.

Then, add the garlic, butter, vegetable broth, shallot and asparagus to the inner pot. Season with salt, pepper, thyme, and rosemary.

Secure the lid. Choose the "Steam" mode and cook for 2 minutes at Low pressure. When cooking is complete, use a quick pressure release and carefully remove the lid.

Serve the sole fillets and garnish with the asparagus and lemon wedges. Enjoy!

Special Scallops with Sour Cream

(Ready in about 15 minutes | Servings 4)

Ingredients

- 1 tablespoon fresh rosemary, chopped
- 1 ½ lb. scallops, peeled and deveined
- 1 tablespoon fresh thyme, chopped
- 2 tablespoons coconut oil, melted
- 1 ½ cup double cream
- 1 celery, chopped
- ½ sour cream
- Sea salt and pepper, to taste
- 1 cup fish broth
- 1 green onion, chopped

Nutritional Information

376 Calories
25.5g Fat
7g Carbs
24.7g Protein
3g Sugars

Directions

Press the "Sauté" button and heat your Instant Pot. Add the coconut oil, fish broth, scallops, celery, salt, pepper, fresh rosemary, fresh thyme, and green onion

Secure the lid. Choose "Manual" mode and Low pressure; cook for 3 minutes. When cooking is complete, use a natural pressure release and carefully remove the lid.

Then, stir in the sour cream and double cream. Close the lid and set to "Warm" for 3-4 minutes.

Serve immediately! Bon appetite!

Nutritious Seafood Bowl

Ingredients

- 1 lb. calamari, cleaned
- 1 leek, diced
- ½ lb. scallops
- 2 tablespoons fresh rosemary, chopped
- 3 garlic cloves, halved
- 2 tablespoons extra-virgin olive oil
- 1/2 lb. lobster
- ½ cup dry white wine
- 1/2 cup red onion, chopped
- 1/2 cup fresh lemon juice
- 1 lb. shrimp, peeled and deveined
- 2 bay leaves
- 2 thyme sprigs
- 3 tomatoes, peeled and chopped
- 1/2 cup black olives, pitted and halved
- 2 tablespoons fresh parsley, chopped
- ½ cup fish broth
- Sea salt and pepper, to taste

Nutritional Information

348 Calories
11.6g Fat
7g Carbs
49.1g Protein
1.6g Sugars

Directions

Add the thyme sprigs, shrimp, sea salt, pepper, calamari, scallops, lobster, bay leaves, fresh rosemary, leek, thyme, white wine, fish broth and garlic to your Instant Pot.

Secure the lid. Choose "Manual" mode and Low pressure; cook for 4 minutes. When cooking is complete, use a quick pressure release and carefully remove the lid.

Drain the seafood and transfer to a large serving bowl.

In a medium bowl combine the lemon juice chopped, tomatoes, olives, parsley, olive oil, red onion, salt, and pepper.

Transfer this mixture to the serving bowl with the seafood. Combine well. Serve and enjoy!

Sicilian Fish Soup

Ingredients

- 2 cloves garlic, minced
- 1/2 lb. salmon, cut into cubes
- 1/2 teaspoon fine sea salt
- 1/2 teaspoon dried grated lemon peel
- 1/3 teaspoon dried marjoram
- 1 carrot, diced
- 1/2 cup scallions, chopped
- 2 tablespoon canola oil
- 10 prawns, peeled
- 1/3 teaspoon dried dill
- 1 celery, diced
- 5 cups vegetable broth

Nutritional Information

211 Calories
14.8g Fat
4.3g Carbs
18.3g Protein
1.3g Sugars

Directions

Press the "Sauté" button and heat the Instant Pot. Add the canola oil and sauté scallions and garlic until fragrant.

Then stir in the salmon cubes, sea salt, dried marjoram, grated lemon peel, carrot, dried dill, celery, prawns and vegetable broth.

Secure the lid. Choose "Manual" mode and High pressure; cook for 5 minutes. When cooking is complete, use a quick pressure release and carefully remove the lid.

Ladle into individual bowls and serve. Bon appétit!

Sardines with Lemon Sauce

Ingredients

- 8 fresh sardines, gutted and cleaned
- 4 tablespoons olive oil
- ½ teaspoon oregano
- 2 tablespoons lemon juice
- 1 bay leaf
- ½ teaspoon chili flakes
- Salt and pepper, to taste
- lemon wedges, for serving
- 1 cup vegetable broth

Nutritional Information

379 Calories
33.8g Fat
5.6g Carbs
15.3g Protein
2.7g Sugars

Directions

Press the "Sauté" button and preheat the Instant Pot. Add the olive oil and sauté the sardines for 30 seconds. If necessary, work in batches.

Then, stir in the oregano, lemon juice, bay leaf, vegetable broth, chili flakes, salt, and pepper.

Secure the lid. Choose "Manual" mode and High pressure; cook for 4 minutes. When cooking is complete, use a quick pressure release and carefully remove the lid.

Serve warm and garnish with lemon wedges. Bon appétit!

VEGETABLES & SIDE DISHES

Friday's Cauliflower Soup

Ingredients

- 1/2 teaspoon paprika
- 3 cloves garlic, minced
- 5 cups vegetable broth
- 4 cups cauliflower
- 3 tablespoons butter
- Salt and pepper, to taste
- 1/2 teaspoon chili powder
- 1 cup heavy cream
- 1 cup cheddar cheese, shredded

Nutritional Information

277 Calories
24.7g Fat
6.6g Carbs
7.9g Protein
4g Sugars

Directions

Preheat your Instant Pot by pressing the "Sauté" button and melt the butter. Saute the onion and garlic until fragrant.

Stir in the cauliflower, vegetable broth, salt, pepper, paprika

Secure the lid. Choose the "Manual" mode and cook for 4 minutes at High pressure. When cooking is complete, use a quick pressure release and carefully remove the lid.

Stir in the heavy cream and cheddar cheese. Let it simmer for 2-3 minutes or until get thick.

Serve warm and add more cheddar on top.

Greenish Brussels Sprouts with Bacon

(Ready in about 10 minutes | Servings 3)

Ingredients

- ½ cup bacon, chopped
- 1 tablespoon olive oil
- 1 teaspoon garlic, minced
- 1 large yellow onion, chopped
- 1 pound Brussels sprouts, washed, trimmed and cut into halves
- Salt and pepper, to taste
- 1/2 teaspoon red pepper flakes
- 1 cup of water

Nutritional Information

219 Calories
15.8g Fat
7g Carbs
8.2g Protein
3.6g Sugars

Directions

Add the steamer basket and 1 cup of water to the inner pot. Place the Brussels sprouts in the steamer basket.

Secure the lid. Choose the "Steam" mode and cook for 3 minutes at High pressure. When cooking is complete, use a quick pressure release and carefully remove the lid. Then drain the water out of the inner pot.

Press the "Sauté" button and heat the olive oil. Saute the garlic, bacon, and onion until aromatic and add the Brussels sprouts. Then, season with salt, pepper, and red pepper flakes. Stir well.

Serve warm! Bon appetite!

Irresistible Kale with Cheese

(Ready in about 10 minutes | Servings 4)

Ingredients

- 1/2 cup scallions, chopped
- ½ teaspoon dried thyme
- 3 garlic cloves, minced
- 1 ½ pounds fresh kale
- 1 cup chicken broth
- ½ teaspoon dried oregano
- 2 tablespoons butter
- 1 cup cream cheese, cubed
- Salt and pepper, to taste

Nutritional Information

440 Calories
31.4g Fat
7g Carbs
24.3 Protein
3.7g Sugars

Directions

Press the "Sauté" button and preheat the Instant Pot. Melt the butter and saute the scallions and garlic until aromatic.

Stir in the chicken broth, dried thyme, kale, dried oregano, cream cheese, salt, and pepper.

Secure the lid. Choose "Manual" mode and High pressure; cook for 2 minutes. When cooking is complete, use a quick pressure release and carefully remove the lid.

Serve warm. Bon appétit!

Family Tomato Soup

Ingredients

- 1 ½ onion, sliced
- 1 celery stalk, diced
- 2 carrots, diced
- 3 cups chicken broth
- Salt and pepper, to taste
- 2 tablespoons fresh basil, chopped
- 1 tablespoon olive oil
- 2 cans tomatoes, diced
- 1/2 cup heavy cream
- ½ cup parmesan cheese, shredded
- 1 tablespoon fresh oregano, chopped

Nutritional Information

235 Calories
13.6g Fat
7g Carbs
6.7 Protein
4.9g Sugars

Directions

Preheat your Instant Pot by pressing the "Sauté" button and heat the olive oil. Add in the garlic, onion, carrots, and celery. Saute for 2-3 minutes. Season with pepper, salt, fresh basil, and fresh oregano.

Stir in the chicken broth and tomato puree. Secure the lid. Choose the "Manual" mode and High pressure; cook for 5 minutes. When cooking is complete, use a quick pressure release and carefully remove the lid.

Then add the heavy cream and seal the lid again. Let it sit for 8 minutes more.

Serve into bowls and top with croutons or with parmesan cheese.

Zucchini with Mayo-Lemon Dressing

(Ready in about 10 minutes | Servings 2)

Ingredients

- 2 tablespoons olive oil
- Salt, to taste
- 1 cup of water
- 4 tablespoons mayonnaise
- 3 medium zucchini, sliced into rings
- ½ teaspoon garlic powder
- ½ teaspoon fresh lemon juice
- fresh basil, for serving

Nutritional Information

235 Calories
23.4g Fat
2g Carbs
5.8 Protein
0.3g Sugars

Directions

Press the "Sauté" button and heat the olive oil. Saute the zucchini until light brown and add 1 cup of water to the inner pot.

Secure the lid. Choose the "Manual" mode and cook for 3 minutes at High pressure. When cooking is complete, use a quick pressure release and carefully remove the lid.

In a small bowl mix the mayonnaise, lemon juice, salt, and garlic powder. Stir well.

Serve the zucchini and top with the dressing. Bon appetite!

Tempting Spinach with Cheese

(Ready in about 10 minutes | Servings 4)

Ingredients

- 2 cloves garlic, minced
- 2 lbs. fresh spinach
- 1/2 cup scallions, chopped
- ½ cup double cream
- ½ cup Monetary jack, shredded
- ½ teaspoon salt
- 2 tablespoons olive oil
- ½ teaspoon pepper
- ½ teaspoon dried rosemary
- 1 cup chicken broth

Nutritional Information

223 Calories
16.2.9g Fat
6.9g Carbs
11.5g Protein
3.3g Sugars

Directions

Press the "Sauté" button and preheat the Instant Pot. Add the olive oil and cook the scallions and garlic until aromatic.

Then stir in the fresh spinach, double cream, monetary jack, salt, pepper, chicken broth, and dried rosemary. Combine well.

Secure the lid. Choose "Manual" mode and High pressure; cook for 2 minutes. When cooking is complete, use a quick pressure release and carefully remove the lid.

Serve warm. Bon appetite!

New Asparagus with Cheddar Cheese

Ingredients

- 2 tablespoons canola oil
- ½ teaspoon salt
- 2 lbs. fresh asparagus
- 1 cup Cheddar cheese, shredded
- ½ teaspoon pepper
- 3 garlic cloves, minced
- 1 cup of water

Nutritional Information

247 Calories
18.4g Fat
7g Carbs
13.1g Protein
4.3g Sugars

Directions

Add to your Instant Pot 1 cup of water and a steamer basket

Place the asparagus on the steamer basket. Then drizzle with canola oil and season with minced garlic, salt, and pepper.

Secure the lid. Choose "Manual" mode and High pressure; cook for 1 minute. When cooking is complete, use a quick pressure release and carefully remove the lid.

Serve warm and top with cheddar cheese. Enjoy!

Fast Porcini Mushrooms with Gouda

Ingredients

- 1 ½ lb. Porcini mushrooms, brushed clean and sliced
- 1 tablespoon avocado oil
- ½ teaspoon salt
- 1/2 cup water
- 1/2 teaspoon dried dill
- 2 tablespoons dry white wine
- 1 cup Gouda cheese
- 2 cloves garlic, minced
- 1 teaspoon dried basil
- ½ teaspoon pepper

Nutritional Information

219 Calories
14.2g Fat
7g Carbs
14.6g Protein
3.8g Sugars

Directions

Press the "Sauté" button and preheat the Instant Pot. Add the avocado oil and cook the garlic until aromatic.

Then add the dried basil, Porcini mushrooms, dried dill, water, dry white wine, pepper, and salt.

Secure the lid. Choose "Manual" mode and Low pressure; cook for 6 minutes. When cooking is complete, use a quick pressure release and carefully remove the lid.

Serve and top with the Gouda cheese. Enjoy!

Red Stuffed Peppers

(Ready in about 15 minutes | Servings 4)

Ingredients

- 2 tablespoons canola oil
- ½ cup scallions chopped, chopped
- 2 garlic cloves, minced
- 1/3 cup mozzarella cheese, shredded
- 1/2 cup cheddar cheese, shredded
- 2 large eggs
- 4 red bell peppers, deveined, tops removed
- 1/2 teaspoon dried oregano
- 1/2 teaspoon dried rosemary
- 1 cup of water

Nutritional Information

255 Calories
15.2g Fat
6.9g Carbs
9.7g Protein
4g Sugars

Directions

Add 1 cup of water and a metal trivet to the Instant Pot.

In a large bowl mix the eggs, garlic, oregano, scallions, rosemary, mozzarella, and cheddar cheese. Stuff the peppers with the cheese mixture.

Place the peppers on the trivet and secure the lid. Choose "Manual" mode and High pressure; cook for 7 minutes. When cooking is complete, use a quick pressure release and carefully remove the lid.

Serve warm. Bon appetite!

Creamy Mushroom Soup

(Ready in about 25 minutes | Servings 4)

Ingredients

- 2 tablespoons butter
- 3 cloves garlic, minced
- 2 shallots, finely chopped
- 1 ½ lb. Cremini mushrooms
- 1 teaspoon dried thyme
- 5 cups vegetable broth
- Salt and ground pepper, to taste
- 1 cup heavy cream
- 1/3 cup fresh parsley, chopped

Nutritional Information

228 Calories
17.8g Fat
7g Carbs
7.1g Protein
4g Sugars

Directions

Preheat your Instant Pot by pressing the "Sauté" button and melt the butter. Cook the garlic, shallot, and thyme until they are aromatic.

Stir in the sliced mushrooms, salt, and pepper. Cook until the mushrooms start to reduce their size.

Pour in the vegetable stock and secure the lid. Choose the "Sealing" mode and High pressure; cook for 10 minutes. Use a quick pressure release for 10 minutes and carefully remove the lid.

When pressure is released, carefully transfer the soup to a blender and blend until smooth consistency.

Transfer the soup into the Instant Pot and stir in the cream. Turn your Instant Pot by pressing the "Sauté" button and leave to simmer for 3-4 minutes or until get thick.

Serve warm and sprinkle with the fresh parsley. Enjoy!

Spectacular Fennel with Goat Cheese

(Ready in about 10 minutes | Servings 3)

Ingredients

- 1 lb. fennel bulbs, cut into wedges
- 2 tablespoons butter, melted
- 1 cup goat cheese, crumbled
- ½ teaspoon dried dill weed
- 2 tablespoons dry white wine
- 1/2 cup vegetable broth
- 1/4 cup of water
- ½ teaspoon salt
- ½ teaspoon pepper

Nutritional Information

313 Calories
22.4g Fat
7g Carbs
13.5g Protein
3.8g Sugars

Directions

Press the "Sauté" button and preheat your Instant Pot. Add the melted butter and saute fennel for 1 minute.

Then, stir in water, salt, pepper, vegetable broth, dry white wine, and dried dill.

Secure the lid. Choose "Manual" mode and Low pressure; cook for 2 minutes. When cooking is complete, use a quick pressure release and carefully remove the lid.

Serve and top with goat cheese. Bon appétit!

FAST SNACKS & APPETIZERS

Party Turkey Skewers

Ingredients

- 1 yellow onion, cut into wedges
- 1/3 cup olives, pitted
- 2 red bell peppers, cut into slices
- ½ cup pickles, cut into circles
- 1 ½ lb. turkey breasts
- 2 tablespoons avocado oil
- 1 tablespoon lemon juice, freshly squeezed
- Salt and pepper, to taste

Nutritional Information

362 Calories
21.8g Fat
4.7g Carbs
38.1g Protein
2.6g Sugars

Directions

Add 1 cup of water and a metal trivet to the Instant Pot. Then arrange the turkey on the metal trivet.

Secure the lid. Choose the "Poultry" mode and High pressure. Cook the chicken for 9 minutes. Once cooking is complete, use a natural pressure release and carefully remove the lid.

Slice the turkey breasts into cubes and season with salt and pepper.

Thread the turkey cubes, yellow onion, olives, pickles, red bell peppers onto bamboo skewers. Drizzle with lemon juice and avocado oil and serve. Enjoy!

Surprising Carrot Meatballs

(Ready in about 15 minutes | Servings 5)

Ingredients

- 1/2 cup Gouda, grated
- 1/2 teaspoon dried dill
- ½ lb. ground chicken
- 2 tablespoons shallots, chopped
- 2 garlic cloves, minced
- 1/3 cup vegetable broth
- 1 large egg, beaten
- 1/2 teaspoon dried oregano
- 2 cups carrot, grated
- 1 tablespoon canola oil
- 1/3 cup parmesan cheese

Nutritional Information

346 Calories
29.2g Fat
6.7g Carbs
15.8g Protein
2.8g Sugars

Directions

In a large bowl mix the ground chicken, Gouda cheese, parmesan cheese, oregano, dill, shallots, garlic, egg, and grated carrots.

Shape the mixture into meatballs.

Press the "Sauté" button and heat the canola oil. Sear your meatballs for 2 minutes, turning them occasionally.

Add the vegetable broth to your Instant Pot and place the meatballs in the liquid.

Secure the lid. Choose "Manual" mode and High pressure; cook for 5 minutes. When cooking is complete, use a quick pressure release; carefully remove the lid.

Serve warm with toothpicks. Bon appétit!

Quick Baby Carrots

Ingredients

- 2 lbs. baby carrots, washed
- 1 cup chicken broth
- 1 ½ tablespoon butter
- 2 tablespoons apple cider
- ½ teaspoon salt
- ½ teaspoon pepper
- 1 teaspoon dried thyme
- 1 tablespoon sesame seeds

Nutritional Information

114 Calories
5.4g Fat
4.7g Carbs
2.6g Protein
3.5 Sugars

Directions

Add baby carrots, chicken broth, butter, apple cider, salt, pepper and dried thyme to your Instant Pot.

Secure the lid. Choose "Manual" mode and High pressure; cook for 3 minutes. When cooking is complete, use a quick pressure release and carefully remove the lid.

Transfer to a serving bowl and sprinkle with sesame seeds. Serve and enjoy!

Spring Prawn Skewers

(Ready in about 10 minutes | Servings 3)

Ingredients

- 1/3 cup water
- 2 tablespoons fresh parsley
- 2 tablespoons soy sauce, chopped
- 3 tablespoons olive oil
- 1/2 teaspoon pepper
- 1 pound prawns, peeled and deveined
- 1/2 teaspoon paprika
- 1 teaspoon minced garlic
- 3 tablespoons fresh lime juice
- ½ teaspoon salt

Nutritional Information

179 Calories
15.7g Fat
3.2g Carbs
4.8g Protein
2.4g Sugars

Directions

In a large bowl mix the soy sauce, olive oil, pepper, salt, garlic, paprika, lime juice, and fresh parsley. Combine well and add the prawns. Refrigerate for 20 minutes.

Then thread the prawns onto metal skewers and add water to your Instant Pot.

Secure the lid. Choose "Manual" mode and High pressure; cook for 1 minute. When cooking is complete, use a quick pressure release and carefully remove the lid.

Arrange the skewers on a serving platter and serve with your favorite Keto sauce. Bon appétit!

Spicy Pork Bites

Ingredients

- 1 lb. pork steak, cut into cubes
- ½ teaspoon dried rosemary
- 1/2 teaspoon red pepper flakes
- 3 tablespoons dry white wine
- 1 teaspoon chili powder
- ½ teaspoon salt
- 1/2 teaspoon dried marjoram
- 1 tablespoon canola oil
- 1/2 teaspoon pepper
- 1 cup vegetable broth
- 1/3 cup parmesan cheese, shredded

Nutritional Information

297 Calories
18.9g Fat
3.8g Carbs
31.4g Protein
1.1g Sugars

Directions

Press the "Sauté" button and heat the canola oil. Cook the pork for 2 minutes.

Then stir in the pepper, salt, red pepper flakes, chili powder, marjoram, vegetable broth, rosemary, and white wine. Combine well.

Secure the lid. Choose "Manual" mode and High pressure; cook for 15 minutes. When cooking is complete, use a natural pressure release and carefully remove the lid.

Serve immediately and sprinkle with parmesan cheese. Bon appétit!

Spring Deviled Eggs
with Bacon

(Ready in about 25 minutes | Servings 4)

Ingredients

- 1 tablespoon green onions, finely chopped
- 1 teaspoon Dijon mustard
- 5 eggs
- 1/3 cup cheddar cheese, shredded
- 2 tablespoons bacon, finely chopped
- 1/2 teaspoon dried dill
- 1/3 cup mayonnaise
- 1 teaspoon red pepper
- ½ teaspoon pepper
- ½ teaspoon salt

Nutritional Information

282 Calories
22.6g Fat
3.1g Carbs
15.3g Protein
1.4g Sugars

Directions

Add 1 cup of water and a steamer basket in your Instant Pot. Arrange the eggs on the steamer basket.

Secure the lid. Choose "Manual" mode and Low pressure; cook for 4 minutes. When cooking is complete, use a quick pressure release and carefully remove the lid.

Leave the eggs to cool for 10 minutes. Then, peel the eggs and slice them into halves.

Place the egg yolks in a bowl along with mayonnaise, Dijon mustard, green onions, cheddar cheese, bacon, dried dill, red pepper, salt, and pepper. Combine well.

Stuff the egg whites with mayo mixture. Serve and enjoy!

Yummy Cheese Dip

Ingredients

- 1 tablespoon fresh chives
- 2 cups cheddar cheese, shredded
- ½ lb. ground beef
- 1 large yellow onion, chopped
- Salt and pepper, to taste
- 1 cup Monetary Jack, shredded
- 2 teaspoons olive oil
- 1 cup vegetable broth

Nutritional Information

402 Calories
38.3g Fat
1.3g Carbs
14.4g Protein
0.8g Sugars

Directions

Press the "Sauté" button and heat your Instant Pot. Add the olive oil and sauté the onion until translucent.

Stir in the ground beef and cook until it is no longer pink. Then add the chili powder, vegetable broth, salt, and pepper.

Secure the lid. Choose "Manual" mode and High pressure. Cook for 4 minutes. When cooking is complete, use a natural pressure release and carefully remove the lid.

Then stir in the cheddar cheese and Monetary Jack cheese. Press again the "Sauté" button and stir until the cheese is melted.

Serve immediately and sprinkle with fresh chives. Bon appétit!

Cocktail Meatballs

(Ready in about 15 minutes | Servings 8)

Ingredients

- 1 lb. ground chicken
- ½ lb. ground pork
- 1 egg, beaten
- 1/2 cup BBQ sauce
- 1/2 cup vegetable broth
- 2 tablespoons fresh parsley, chopped
- 1 teaspoon garlic, minced
- 1 cup Romano cheese, shredded
- 2 teaspoons avocado oil
- 2 tablespoons fresh scallions, chopped
- 1/2 cup Parmesan cheese, grated
- Salt and pepper, to your taste

Nutritional Information

320 Calories
22.3g Fat
3.2g Carbs
24.6g Protein
1.3g Sugars

Directions

In a large bowl mix the ground chicken, ground turkey, egg, parmesan cheese, Romano cheese, fresh parsley, fresh scallions, garlic, salt and pepper. Combine well and shape the mixture into balls.

Press the "Sauté" button and heat the avocado oil. Sear the meatballs for a few minutes and pour in the vegetable broth and BBQ sauce.

Secure the lid. Choose the "Manual" setting and cook for 7 minutes under High pressure. When cooking is complete, use a quick pressure release and carefully remove the lid.

Serve the meatballs and top with the sauce. Bon appétit!

Healthy Asparagus

Ingredients

- 1 bunch of fresh asparagus, trimmed
- 1/2 cup chicken broth
- ½ teaspoon salt
- 2 tablespoons butter
- 1/2 teaspoon pepper
- 1/3 cup water
- 1/3 cup shallots, chopped
- ½ cup parmesan cheese, grated

Nutritional Information

68 Calories
9.4g Fat
5.8g Carbs
6.6g Protein
2.8g Sugars

Directions

- Press the "Sauté" button and heat your Instant Pot. Then melt the butter and sauté the shallots until tender.
- Stir in the asparagus, salt, pepper, water, and chicken broth.
- Secure the lid. Choose "Manual" mode and High pressure. Cook for 2 minutes. When cooking is complete, use a quick pressure release and carefully remove the lid.
- Transfer the asparagus to a serving platter and top with parmesan cheese. Serve with your favorite dip and enjoy!

Stuffed Mushrooms with Pancetta and Cheddar

(Ready in about 10 minutes | Servings 3)

Ingredients

- 9 large white mushrooms, stems removed
- 1/2 teaspoon dried rosemary
- 1 ½ cup pancetta, chopped
- 2 tablespoons fresh parsley, finely chopped
- 1 ½ tablespoon olive oil
- 1 ½ cup cheddar cheese, shredded
- 2 cloves garlic, minced
- 1/2 teaspoon dried oregano
- ½ teaspoon salt
- 1 shallot, chopped
- ½ teaspoon pepper
- 1 cup of water

Nutritional Information

372 Calories
31.2g Fat
5.3g Carbs
17.9g Protein
2.3g Sugars

Directions

Press the "Sauté" button and preheat your Instant Pot. Add the olive oil and sauté the shallots until tender.

Stir in the garlic and cook until aromatic. Now, add the pancetta, fresh parsley, cheddar cheese, dried oregano, dried rosemary, salt, and pepper.

Then, fill the mushroom caps with this mixture.

Add 1 cup of water and a steamer basket to you Instant Pot. Place the stuffed mushrooms in the steamer basket.

Secure the lid. Choose "Manual" mode and High pressure; cook for 6 minutes. When cooking is complete, use a quick pressure release and carefully remove the lid.

Serve warm. Bon appetite!

Cauliflower Medley with Ham

(Ready in about 15 minutes | Servings 3)

Ingredients

- 1 cup ham, chopped
- 1 cup double cream
- 1 large yellow onion, chopped
- 1 cup cauliflower, broken into florets
- ½ teaspoon salt
- ½ teaspoon pepper
- 1/2 cup Monetary Jack cheese, shredded
- 2 cloves garlic, minced
- 1 tablespoon sesame oil
- 1/2 teaspoon red pepper flakes, crushed
- 2 tablespoons fresh chives, finely chopped
- 1 1/2 cup water

Nutritional Information

384 Calories
31.3g Fat
6.8g Carbs
17.6g Protein
3.8g Sugars

Directions

Press the "Sauté" button to preheat your Instant Pot. Add the sesame oil and cook the garlic and onion until aromatic.

Stir in the cauliflower, ham, water, salt, pepper, double cream, and red pepper flakes.

Secure the lid. Choose "Manual" mode and High pressure; cook for 5 minutes. When cooking is complete, use a natural pressure release and carefully remove the lid.

Press the "Sauté" button and top with Monetary Jack cheese. Simmer for 2-3 minutes.

Garnish with fresh chives and serve. Enjoy!

Non-Traditional Eggplant and Ground Beef Bowl

Ingredients

- 1/2 teaspoon turmeric powder
- 1 yellow onion, chopped
- ½ lb. ground beef
- 2 medium eggplants, peeled and sliced
- 4 garlic cloves, minced
- 1 teaspoon red pepper flakes
- 1 cup vegetable broth
- 1 tablespoon avocado oil
- ½ teaspoon salt
- ½ teaspoon pepper
- 1 cup mozzarella cheese, shredded
- ½ teaspoon dried basil
- 1 ½ cup tomatoes, puréed

Nutritional Information

510 Calories
39.5g Fat
7g Carbs
15.8g Protein
4g Sugars

Directions

Press the "Sauté" button and preheat your Instant Pot. Add the avocado oil. Cook the garlic and onion until translucent.

Stir in the ground beef and cook for 2-3 minutes or until no longer pink. Then, add the eggplants, turmeric powder, red pepper flakes, vegetable broth, pureed tomatoes, salt, pepper, and dried basil.

Secure the lid. Choose "Poultry" mode and High pressure; cook for 9 minutes. When cooking is complete, use a natural pressure release and carefully remove the lid.

Serve immediately and top with shredded mozzarella cheese. Bon appétit!

EGGS & DAIRY

Excellent Spinach Frittata

(Ready in about 15 minutes | Servings 3)

Ingredients

- 2 cups fresh spinach, washed and chopped
- ½ cup scallions, chopped
- 1 teaspoon red pepper flakes
- 1 red bell pepper, chopped
- ½ teaspoon salt
- 1/2 teaspoon pepper
- 6 eggs, whisked
- 1 teaspoon garlic powder
- 2 tablespoons butter, melted
- ½ teaspoon dried basil
- 1 teaspoon dried chives
- 1 Roma tomato, chopped
- 1 cup of water

Nutritional Information

210 Calories
10.9g Fat
4.1g Carbs
5.3g Protein
2.8g Sugars

Directions

In a large baking pan add the melted butter. Set aside.

Then, in a large bowl combine the eggs, fresh spinach, tomatoes, scallions, red bell pepper, salt, pepper, dried chives, dried basil, garlic powder, and red pepper flakes.

Spoon the mixture into the prepared baking pan and cover with a sheet of foil.

Add a metal trivet and 1 cup of water and to the Instant Pot. Lower the baking pan onto the trivet.

Secure the lid. Choose "Manual" mode and Low pressure; cook for 7 minutes. When cooking is complete, use a natural pressure release and carefully remove the lid.

Serve immediately. Bon appétit!

Fluffy Eggs with Bacon

Ingredients

- 4 slices of bacon, chopped
- 2 tablespoons light cream
- 1 tablespoon butter, melted
- ½ teaspoon salt
- 1/3 teaspoon pepper
- 4 eggs, beaten
- 1/2 teaspoon smoked paprika
- 1/3 cup fresh chives chopped
- 1/3 cup parmesan cheese, shredded
- 1 cup of water

Nutritional Information

425 Calories
35.3g Fat
4.1g Carbs
22.4g Protein
0.6g Sugars

Directions

Add a metal rack and 1 cup of water to the Instant Pot.

In a large bowl add the eggs, bacon, chives, light cream, salt, pepper, smoked paprika, and parmesan cheese. Mix well.

Spritz a heatproof bowl with a nonstick cooking spray. Then, spoon the mixture into the prepared bowl and lower the bowl onto the rack.

Secure the lid. Choose "Manual" mode and Low pressure; cook for 7 minutes. When cooking is complete, use a natural pressure release and carefully remove the lid.

Serve warm and enjoy!

Egg Muffins with Ham

Ingredients

- ½ cup ham, finely sliced
- 2 tablespoons milk
- ½ teaspoon salt
- 1/3 teaspoon pepper
- 5 eggs, whisked
- 1/2 cup scallions, chopped
- 1/2 cup Emmental cheese, grated
- 1 cup of water

Nutritional Information

243 Calories
17.8 Fat
2.9g Carbs
18.7g Protein
0.9g Sugars

Directions

Add 1 cup of water and a metal rack to the Instant Pot.

In a bowl mix the eggs, ham, salt, pepper, scallions, double cream, and Emmental cheese.

Then, fill in the silicone muffin cups and place them on the rack.

Secure the lid. Choose "Manual" mode and High pressure; cook for 6 minutes. When cooking is complete, use a natural pressure release and carefully remove the lid.

Serve warm and enjoy!

Rich Casserole with Cheddar Cheese

(Ready in about 25 minutes | Servings 4)

Ingredients

- 2 zucchinis, cut into circles
- 1 cup pancetta, sliced
- 1 cup Cremini mushrooms, sliced
- 6 eggs
- ½ cup milk
- 1 cup cheddar cheese, shredded
- ½ teaspoon salt
- ½ teaspoon pepper
- 1 cup of water

Nutritional Information

409 Calories
29.7g Fat
6.4g Carbs
28.2g Protein
3.2g Sugars

Directions

Add 1 cup of water and a metal trivet to the Instant Pot.

Spritz a baking dish that fits inside your Instant Pot with a nonstick cooking spray.

Place the zucchini on the bottom of the dish and add the Cremini mushrooms on the top.

In a bowl, mix the eggs, milk, cheddar cheese, salt, pancetta, and pepper. Spoon this mixture over the top.

Then, lower the baking pan onto the trivet.

Secure the lid. Choose "Manual" mode and High pressure; cook for 16 minutes. When cooking is complete, use a natural pressure release and carefully remove the lid.

Leave to cool and serve. Bon appétit!

Stuffed Avocado Boats

(Ready in about 10 minutes | Servings 2)

Ingredients

- 4 eggs
- 4 tablespoons Monetary Jack cheese, grated
- 2 avocados, pitted and cut into halves
- 1 tablespoon fresh lemon juice
- 1 teaspoon paprika
- Salt and pepper, to taste

Nutritional Information

476 Calories
36.6g Fat
6.9g Carbs
28.4g Protein
2.4g Sugars

Directions

Add 1 cup of water and a steamer basket to your Instant Pot.

Line the steamer basket with aluminum foil.

Then, remove with a spoon some of the avocado flesh and set it aside for another use.

Arrange the avocado halves on your steamer basket. Place an egg to each avocado and season with salt, pepper, and paprika. Top with the shredded cheese.

Secure the lid. Choose "Manual" mode and High pressure; cook for 4 minutes. When cooking is complete, use a natural pressure release and carefully remove the lid.

Serve warm and drizzle with fresh lemon juice! Enjoy!

Elementary Deviled Eggs

Ingredients

- 1/3 cup mayonnaise
- 1 tablespoon avocado oil
- 1 ½ teaspoon Dijon mustard
- 8 eggs
- 1 tablespoon fresh lemon juice
- 1 ½ teaspoon smoked paprika
- ½ teaspoon salt
- 1/3 teaspoon pepper

Nutritional Information

369 Calories
28.7g Fat
3.2g Carbs
23g Protein
0.3g Sugars

Directions

Add water and a steamer basket to the Instant Pot.

Arrange the eggs in a steamer basket if you have one.

Secure the lid. Choose "Manual" mode and High pressure; cook for 6 minutes. When cooking is complete, use a natural pressure release and carefully remove the lid.

Leave the eggs to cool. Peel the eggs and separate egg whites from yolks. Set aside,

Then, in a large bowl stir in the mayonnaise, mustard, salt, pepper, fresh lemon juice, and reserved egg yolks. Combine well

Arrange the stuffed eggs on a serving platter. Sprinkle paprika over eggs and serve. Bon appetite!

Delicious Cheese Soup

Ingredients

- 1 carrot, chopped
- ½ teaspoon onion powder
- 1 teaspoon basil
- 1/2 cup cheddar cheese, shredded
- 1/2 cup leeks, chopped
- 5 cups vegetable stock
- ½ cup heavy cream
- 2 celery stalks, chopped
- ½ teaspoon salt
- ½ teaspoon pepper
- 11/2 tablespoon fresh parsley, chopped
- 2 tablespoons avocado oil
- 1/2 teaspoon oregano
- ½ teaspoon garlic powder
- 3/4 cup Monetary Jack cheese, shredded

Nutritional Information

298 Calories
24.6g Fat
6.g Carbs
10.1g Protein
2.9g Sugars

Directions

Press the "Sauté" button and preheat your Instant Pot. Add the avocado oil and saute the leeks until fragrant.

Stir in the celery, oregano, garlic powder, salt, carrot, vegetable broth, basil, pepper, and onion powder.

Secure the lid. Choose "Manual" mode and High pressure; cook for 15 minutes. When cooking is complete, use a natural pressure release and carefully remove the lid.

Add the cheddar cheese, heavy cream, and Monetary Jack cheese. Stir, and press the "Sauté" button one more time. Then, cook the soup for a couple of minutes longer or until thoroughly heated.

Serve warm and top with fresh parsley! Bon appetite!

Four-Cheese Dip

Ingredients

- 1/2 teaspoon garlic powder
- 1/3 cup blue cheese, crumbled
- ½ cup Monterey-Jack cheese, shredded
- 1/2 cup vegetable broth
- ½ cup cooked bacon, chopped
- 1 cup Cheddar cheese, shredded
- 1 ½ tablespoon fresh chives, roughly chopped
- ½ cup Gouda cheese, shredded

Nutritional Information

203 Calories
20.1g Fat
0.9g Carbs
6.1g Protein
0.1g Sugars

Directions

Add the vegetable broth, bacon, Cheddar cheese, Monetary Jack cheese, garlic powder, blue cheese, and Gouda cheese to the Instant Pot.

Press the "Sauté" button and preheat your Instant Pot. Stir until everything is well combined and warm.

Sprinkle with fresh chopped chives and serve. Enjoy!

Fancy Mini Frittatas

(Ready in about 15 minutes | Servings 4)

Ingredients

- 1 cup Pepperoni sausage, chopped
- 1/4 teaspoon pepper
- 5 eggs
- 1/2 cup scallions, chopped
- 1/2 teaspoon garlic powder
- 1/2 teaspoon dried dill weed
- 1/2 cup full-fat milk
- ½ teaspoon salt
- ½ teaspoon onion powder
- 1 cup of water

Nutritional Information

219 Calories
16.7g Fat
4.2g Carbs
14.2g Protein
2.4g Sugars

Directions

Add 1 cup of water and a metal trivet to the bottom of the inner pot.

In a large bowl mix the eggs, onion powder, salt, pepper, garlic powder, dried dill, milk, scallions, and chopped pepperoni. Combine well and spoon the mixture into silicone molds.

Lower the silicone molds onto the trivet.

Secure the lid. Choose "Manual" mode and High pressure; cook for 8 minutes. When cooking is complete, use a quick pressure release and carefully remove the lid. Bon appétit!

Simple Eggs with Mortadella

(Ready in about 10 minutes | Servings 3)

Ingredients

- 6 large eggs
- 6 slices mortadella
- 2 tablespoons fresh chives, finely chopped
- ½ teaspoons salt
- ½ teaspoon red pepper

Nutritional Information

204 Calories
17.2g Fat
2.2g Carbs
10.7g Protein
0.2g Sugars

Directions

Add 1 cup of water and a metal trivet to the Instant Pot.

Spritz six silicone cups with a nonstick cooking spray.

Place a slice of mortadella to the bottom into each cup and crack an egg on the top.

Then, lower the silicone cups onto the metal trivet.

Secure the lid. Choose "Steam" mode and High pressure; cook for 3 minutes. When cooking is complete, use a quick pressure release and carefully remove the lid.

Season your eggs with red pepper and salt. Bon appétit!

Classic Eggs with Tomato Sauce

Ingredients

- 2 tablespoons sesame oil
- 1 large onion, diced
- 2 garlic cloves, minced
- 2 red bell peppers, diced
- 1 green bell pepper, diced
- ½ teaspoon salt
- ½ teaspoon pepper
- 1 teaspoon paprika
- 1 teaspoon dried basil
- 1 ½ can crushed tomatoes
- 5 eggs
- 2 tablespoons fresh parsley, chopped

Nutritional Information

269 Calories
19.3g Fat
5.9g Carbs
13.2g Protein
4.1g Sugars

Directions

Press the "Sauté" button and preheat your Instant Pot. Add the sesame oil and saute the garlic and onion aromatic.

Stir in the green and red peppers, tomatoes, basil, paprika, salt, and pepper.

Then, crack the eggs into the vegetable mixture.

Secure the lid. Choose "Manual" mode and Low pressure; cook for 6 minutes. When cooking is complete, use a quick pressure release and carefully remove the lid.

Serve warm and top with fresh parsley. Enjoy!

Afternoon Lettuce Sandwiches

Ingredients

- 5 eggs, whisked
- 1/3 cup whipped cream
- ½ cup cheddar cheese
- ½ cup scallion, finely chopped
- 1/3 teaspoon paprika
- ½ teaspoon salt
- ½ teaspoon pepper
- 8 leaves of Iceberg lettuce
- For the Mayo sauce:
- 1 teaspoon Sriracha
- 5 tablespoons mayonnaise
- 1 teaspoon mustard
- 1 ½ teaspoon dried oregano

Nutritional Information

327 Calories
26.7g Fat
4.6g Carbs
16.8g Protein
2.2g Sugars

Directions

Add 1 cup of water and a metal rack to your Instant Pot. Then, spritz a baking dish with a nonstick cooking spray.

In a large bowl combine the eggs, whipped cream, paprika, salt, pepper, scallion, and cheddar cheese.

Spoon the mixture into the baking dish.

Secure the lid. Choose "Manual" mode and High pressure; cook for 3 minutes. When cooking is complete, use a natural pressure release; carefully remove the lid.

Meanwhile, in a small bowl mix all the ingredients for the mayo sauce. Stir well.

Divide the egg mixture among the lettuce leaves and top with the mayo sauce. Wrap each leaf, and serve immediately. Bon appétit!

VEGAN

Marvelous Portobello Mushrooms

Ingredients

- 2 garlic cloves, minced
- 1 teaspoon dried rosemary
- 2 lbs. Portobello mushrooms, cleaned and sliced
- 1 teaspoon dried basil
- 1 cup vegetable broth
- 2 tablespoons olive oil
- 1 large yellow onion
- ½ teaspoon pepper
- ½ teaspoon dried thyme
- ½ teaspoon salt

Nutritional Information

127 Calories
7.9g Fat
4.2g Carbs
8.4g Protein
3.2g Sugars

Directions

Press the "Sauté" button and preheat your Instant Pot. Add the olive oil and cook onion and garlic until aromatic.

Then stir in the sliced mushrooms, salt, pepper, dried rosemary, dried thyme, dried basil and vegetable broth.

Secure the lid. Choose "Manual" mode and Low pressure; cook for 4 minutes. When cooking is complete, use a quick pressure release and carefully remove the lid.

Serve and enjoy!

Green Spinach Stew

Ingredients

- 2 tablespoons sesame oil
- 1 yellow onion, sliced
- 3 cloves garlic, minced
- ½ teaspoon pepper
- ½ teaspoon salt
- 1 1/2 cup coconut cream
- 1 teaspoon turmeric powder
- 6 cups fresh spinach, washed
- 1 celery stalk, chopped
- 2 tablespoons dry white wine
- 1 cup vegetable broth
- ½ teaspoon chili powder

Directions

- Press the "Sauté" button and preheat your Instant Pot. Add the sesame oil and cook onion and garlic until aromatic.
- Then, place all of the above ingredients in the Instant Pot.
- Secure the lid. Choose "Manual" mode and High pressure; cook for 5 minutes. When cooking is complete, use a quick pressure release and carefully remove the lid.
- Serve warm. Bon appétit!

Nutritional Information

226 Calories
18.7g Fat
7g Carbs
7.9g Protein
1.3g Sugars

Peppery Broccoli

Ingredients

- 1/2 cup water
- 1 ½ lb. broccoli, broken into florets
- 1 tablespoon fresh coriander, chopped
- 3 cloves garlic, pressed
- 1 teaspoon curry powder
- 2 scallions, chopped
- 1/2 teaspoon ground cumin
- 2 tablespoons avocado oil
- 1 red chili pepper, minced
- 1 tablespoon lemon juice
- 1 1/2 tablespoon Sriracha sauce
- Salt and pepper, to taste

Nutritional Information

120 Calories
8.9g Fat
6.5g Carbs
7.7g Protein
2.4g Sugars

Directions

Press the "Sauté" button and preheat your Instant Pot. Add the avocado oil and sauté the scallions and garlic until aromatic.

Stir in the curry powder, cumin, salt, pepper, broccoli, Sriracha sauce, lemon juice, fresh coriander, water, and red chili pepper.

Secure the lid. Choose "Manual" mode and High pressure; cook for 3 minutes. When cooking is complete, use a quick pressure release and carefully remove the lid.

Serve immediately. Bon appétit!

Marinated Vegan Cauliflower

Ingredients

- 1 teaspoon onion powder
- 1 head cauliflower, cut into florets
- 1 cup of water
- 2 tablespoons sesame oil
- 1/2 teaspoon dried dill weed
- ½ teaspoon dried thyme
- 2 teaspoons lemon juice
- 1 teaspoon garlic powder
- 1 teaspoon paprika
- 2 tablespoons soy sauce
- Salt and pepper, to taste

Nutritional Information

112 Calories
9.1g Fat
6.9g Carbs
3.8g Protein
2.6g Sugars

Directions

In a large bowl mix the sesame oil, paprika, salt, pepper, dried dill, dried thyme, lemon juice, garlic powder, onion powder, paprika, and soy sauce. Combine well.

Add the cauliflower florets to the marinate and soak well.

Then, add 1 cup of water and a steamer basket to your Instant Pot. Transfer the cauliflower florets in the steamer basket

Secure the lid. Choose "Manual" mode and High pressure; cook for 1 minute. When cooking is complete, use a quick pressure release and carefully remove the lid.

Serve warm and enjoy!

Zucchini with Barbecue Sauce

(Ready in about 10 minutes | Servings 4)

Ingredients

- 1 ½ lb. zucchini, sliced
- For the Barbecue sauce:
- 1 can tomato paste
- 1 cup of water
- ½ teaspoon salt
- ½ teaspoon pepper
- 3 tablespoons avocado oil
- 1/2 teaspoon porcini powder
- 1 teaspoon smoked pepper
- 1 teaspoon onion powder
- 1 teaspoon garlic powder
- 11/2 teaspoon mustard seeds
- 2 tablespoons lemon juice
- A few drops liquid Stevia

Directions

Press the "Sauté" button and preheat your Instant Pot.

Add the tomato paste, water, salt, pepper, onion powder, porcini powder, garlic powder, smoked pepper, avocado oil, lemon juice, stevia, and mustard seeds. Combine well.

Secure the lid. Choose "Manual" mode and High pressure; cook for 4 minutes. When cooking is complete, use a natural pressure release and carefully remove the lid.

Serve warm. Enjoy!

Nutritional Information

99 Calories
8.1g Fat
6.9g Carbs
7.8g Protein
3g Sugars

The Best Italian Peppers

Ingredients

- 3 garlic cloves, minced
- 1 jalapeno pepper, finely chopped
- 1 teaspoon paprika
- 2 tomatoes, pureed
- 1/3 cup dry white wine
- 1/2 teaspoon dried oregano
- 1 red bell pepper, seeded and chopped
- 1 celery stalk, chopped
- 1/2 cup onion, chopped
- 1 green bell pepper, seeded and chopped
- 1 ½ teaspoon dried basil
- ½ cup vegetable broth
- 2 tablespoons coconut oil
- 1 yellow bell pepper, seeded and chopped
- 2 tablespoons fresh basil, finely chopped
- Salt and pepper, to taste

Directions

Press the "Sauté" button and preheat your Instant Pot. Add the coconut oil and sauté the garlic and onion until aromatic.

Stir in red pepper, salt, pepper, vegetable broth, yellow peppers, paprika, dry white wine, green peppers, oregano, basil, tomatoes, celery, and jalapeno pepper.

Secure the lid. Choose "Manual" mode and High pressure; cook for 3 minutes. When cooking is complete, use a quick pressure release and carefully remove the lid.

Serve into bowls and top with fresh basil and mozzarella. Bon appétit!

Nutritional Information

142 Calories
11.2g Fat
7g Carbs
8.5g Protein
3.9g Sugars

Powerful Green Beans with Zucchini

(Ready in about 10 minutes | Servings 3)

Ingredients

- 2 tablespoons sesame oil
- 1/3 cup scallions, chopped
- 2 medium zucchini, peeled and sliced
- 2 cloves garlic, minced
- ½ lb. green beans
- 1 teaspoon cumin
- 1 teaspoon dried oregano
- 3 tablespoons tomato paste
- 1/2 cup vegetable broth
- Salt and pepper, to taste
- 1 teaspoon red pepper flakes, crushed

Nutritional Information

106 Calories
9.8g Fat
6.7g Carbs
3.3g Protein
2.8g Sugars

Directions

Press the "Sauté" button and preheat your Instant Pot. Add the sesame oil and sauté scallions and garlic until aromatic.

Stir in the zucchini, green beans, vegetable broth, salt, pepper, tomato paste cumin, red pepper, and oregano.

Secure the lid. Choose "Manual" mode and Low pressure; cook for 3 minutes. When cooking is complete, use a quick pressure release and carefully remove the lid.

Serve immediately and enjoy!

Vegan Broccoli Soup

Ingredients

- 1 teaspoon dried chervil
- 1 head broccoli, broken into florets
- 2 teaspoons olive oil
- ½ cup green onion, chopped
- 5 cups of water
- 1 teaspoon fresh parsley, chopped
- 1/2 cup coconut milk, unsweetened
- 2 cloves garlic, minced
- 1 celery stalk, chopped
- 1 teaspoon dried tarragon
- Salt and pepper, to taste

Nutritional Information

79 Calories
4.6g Fat
3.1g Carbs
3.8g Protein
1.5g Sugars

Directions

Press the "Sauté" button and preheat your Instant Pot. Heat the olive oil and sauté garlic and green onion until tender.

Stir in the broccoli, dried chervil, celery, water, fresh parsley, salt, dried tarragon pepper.

Secure the lid. Choose "Manual" mode and Low pressure; cook for 4 minutes. When cooking is complete, use a quick pressure release and carefully remove the lid.

Then, add the coconut milk and press the "Sauté" button again. Let it simmer for 4 minutes more.

Purée the soup with an immersion blender until smooth and return the soup to the Instant Pot.

Serve into soup bowls and serve warm. Bon appétit!

Silk Mushroom Purée

Ingredients

- 1 lb. Cremini mushrooms, without stems
- 1/2 teaspoon garlic powder
- 2 tablespoons coconut oil
- 1/3 cup vegetable broth
- 1/2 teaspoon onion powder
- 1 teaspoon dried thyme
- 1/3 cup coconut cream
- ½ teaspoon salt
- 1/2 teaspoon pepper

Nutritional Information

319 Calories
32.7g Fat
4.1g Carbs
6.2g Protein
2.4g Sugars

Directions

Add the mushrooms, salt, pepper, garlic powder, vegetable broth, onion powder, coconut oil, and dried thyme your Instant Pot.

Secure the lid. Choose "Manual" mode and High pressure; cook for 4 minutes. When cooking is complete, use a quick pressure release and carefully remove the lid.

Transfer the mushroom mixture to your food processor and add coconut cream. Purée the mixture until smooth. Serve warm. Bon appétit!

New Broccoli Balls with Hemp

Ingredients

- 1 large head broccoli, broken into florets
- 2 teaspoons vegan margarine
- 1/3 cup coconut cream
- 1 garlic clove, minced
- 3 tablespoons Kalamata olives, pitted
- 1 teaspoon smoked paprika
- 3 tablespoons hemp seeds
- 1/3 cup vegan parmesan
- Salt and pepper, to taste

Nutritional Information

123 Calories
10.4g Fat
3.8g Carbs
4.9g Protein
1.2g Sugars

Directions

Add a steamer basket and 1 cup of water in your Instant Pot. Arrange the broccoli in the steamer basket.

Secure the lid. Choose "Manual" mode and High pressure; cook for 2 minutes. When cooking is complete, use a quick pressure release and carefully remove the lid.

In a food processor add the broccoli, paprika, vegan parmesan, salt, pepper, vegan margarine, Kalamata olives, garlic, and coconut cream. Puree until smooth.

Form the mixture into balls and roll each ball into hemp seeds. Arrange on a nice serving platter and enjoy!

DESSERTS

Great Strawberry Curd

Ingredients

- 1/3 cup unsalted butter
- ½ cup Swerve
- 4 egg yolks, beaten
- 1 teaspoon grated lemon zest
- 1/2 teaspoon vanilla extract
- 1 cup fresh strawberry, pureed

Nutritional Information

320 Calories
29.6g Fat
1.4g Carbs
8.9g Protein
3.9g Sugars

Directions

Blend the unsalted butter and Swerve in a food processor. Stir in the eggs and blend for 1 minute longer.

Then, add the strawberries, lemon zest, and vanilla. Divide the mixture among four Mason jars and cover them with lids.

Add 2 cups of water and a metal rack to the Instant Pot. Lower your jars onto the rack.

Secure the lid. Choose "Manual" mode and High pressure; cook for 13 minutes. When cooking is complete, use a natural pressure release and carefully remove the lid.

Leave to cool in your refrigerator and serve. Bon appétit!

Light Cacao Pudding

Ingredients

- 1/2 cup Swerve
- 1 teaspoon vanilla
- 1 ½ cup milk
- 5 egg yolks
- ½ cup water
- 1 cup heavy cream
- 1/3 cup cacao
- ½ teaspoon salt

Nutritional Information

231 Calories
19.7g Fat
5.4g Carbs
7.8g Protein
4.5g Sugars

Directions

Place a metal trivet into your Instant Pot and add ½ cup of water.

Heat a large saucepan and stir in the milk, heavy cream, and vanilla. Simmer for 3-4 minutes.

Then combine in a large bowl the egg yolks, Swerve, cacao, and salt. Slowly add the cacao mixture into the egg mixture.

Pour the mixture into jars. Place the jars onto the trivet.

Secure the lid. Choose the "Manual" mode and cook for 6 minutes at High pressure. When cooking is complete, use a natural pressure release and carefully remove the lid.

Take out the jars and leave to cool. Serve and enjoy!

Mixed Berries Cobbler

(Ready in about 20 minutes | Servings 4)

Ingredients

- 1 cup almond flour
- 1/3 cup coconut flour
- 1/2 cup Swerve
- 1 teaspoon baking soda
- 1/2 cup coconut cream
- 1 cup of water
- 1/3 cup butter, melted
- 1/2 teaspoon vanilla
- 1/2 cup fresh raspberries
- 1/3 cup fresh blueberries

Nutritional Information

222 Calories
18.6g Fat
6.7g Carbs
8.9g Protein
5g Sugars

Directions

Add 1 cup of water and a metal trivet to your Instant Pot.

In a large bowl mix the almond flour, coconut flour, baking soda, Swerve, coconut cream, and vanilla. Spoon the mixture into a baking pan, lightly greased with butter.

Fold in blueberries and raspberries. Stir to combine. Lower the baking dish onto the trivet.

Secure the lid. Choose "Bean/Chili" mode and High pressure; cook for 13 minutes. When cooking is complete, use a natural pressure release and carefully remove the lid.

Leave to cool and serve. Bon appétit!

Fabulous Coconut and Pistachio Crème

Ingredients

- 1 cup of coconut milk
- 2 tablespoons gelatin
- 4 eggs
- 1 teaspoon vanilla extract
- 1 ½ cup heavy whipping cream
- 2 tablespoons coconut flakes
- 1/3 cup pistachio, finely chopped
- 2 tablespoons cacao powder
- 2 cups of water
- 1/3 cup Swerve

Nutritional Information

329 Calories
26.4g Fat
6.9g Carbs
12.3g Protein
4.9g Sugars

Directions

Add 2 cups of water and a metal rack to your Instant Pot.

In a food processor add the eggs, Swerve, vanilla, coconut milk, whipping cream, pistachio, gelatin, cacao powder and coconut flakes.

Blend the cream, water, eggs, Swerve, almond extract, vanilla extract, and almonds in your food processor.

Divide the mixture between four Mason jars and cover your jars with lids. Lower the jars onto the rack.

Secure the lid. Choose "Manual" mode and High pressure; cook for 8 minutes. When cooking is complete, use a natural pressure release and carefully remove the lid.

Leave to cool and enjoy!

Popular Raspberry Porridge

Ingredients

- 5 tablespoons golden flax meal
- 6 tablespoons coconut flour
- 1 ½ cup water
- 1/3 teaspoon salt
- 4 eggs, whisked
- 1/3 cup butter
- 6 tablespoons double cream
- 1 ½ cup raspberries

Nutritional Information

316 Calories
24g Fat
6.9g Carbs
9.1g Protein
3.9g Sugars

Directions

Place the coconut flour, water, eggs, butter, raspberries, double cream, salt and golden flax to the Instant Pot.

Secure the lid. Choose "Manual" mode and High pressure; cook for 6 minutes. When cooking is complete, use a quick pressure release and carefully remove the lid.

Serve and enjoy!

Tea Almond Cookies

Ingredients

- 1 cup almond flour
- 1/2 cup Swerve
- 1 teaspoon baking powder
- ½ teaspoon salt
- 1 tablespoon sesame oil
- 1/2 teaspoon ground cinnamon
- 2 eggs, whisked
- 1 teaspoon vanilla extract
- 1 teaspoon almond extract
- 1/3 cup almonds, finely chopped

Nutritional Information

123 Calories
6.1g Fat
3.2g Carbs
5.9g Protein
0.2g Sugars

Directions

In a large bowl mix the salt, baking powder, almond flour, Swerve, and cinnamon. Combine well.

In a separate bowl combine the vanilla, almond extract, sesame oil, eggs, and finely chopped almonds. Then, add wet mixture to the dry mixture.

Add 1 cup of water to the Instant Pot. Then, pour the mixture into well-greased idli molds and lower it onto the bottom of your Instant Pot.

Secure the lid. Choose "Manual" mode and Low pressure; cook for 14 minutes. When cooking is complete, use a natural pressure release and carefully remove the lid.

Store in an airtight container. Enjoy!

Espresso Souffle

Ingredients

- 1/2 cup double cream
- ½ cup whipping cream
- 1/3 cup butter, melted
- 1 teaspoon ground cinnamon
- 1 teaspoon vanilla extract
- 3 tablespoons cocoa powder, unsweetened
- 1 tablespoon instant coffee granules
- 1/4 cup coconut flour
- ½ teaspoon salt
- ½ teaspoon nutmeg, grated
- 3 eggs plus 2 egg yolks
- 1/2 cup Swerve
- 2 cups of water

Nutritional Information

319 Calories
21.3g Fat
5.1g Carbs
8.9g Protein
1.9g Sugars

Directions

Add 2 cups of water and a metal rack to your Instant Pot. Spritz a soufflé dish with a non-stick cooking spray.

In a large bowl mix the coconut flour, salt, cocoa powder, and cinnamon.

Then, in another bowl add the eggs, Swerve, nutmeg, melted butter, double cream and whipping cream. Mix.

Gradually add the egg mixture to the dry mixture. Combine well.

Pour the batter into the prepared soufflé dish.

Secure the lid. Choose "Manual" mode and Low pressure; cook for 22 minutes. When cooking is complete, use a natural pressure release and carefully remove the lid.

Leave to cool and serve. Bon appétit!

Old-Fashioned Carrot Cake

Ingredients

- ½ teaspoon salt
- 1/2 cup Swerve, powdered
- 1/2 lb. carrot, peeled and shredded
- 3 eggs, beaten
- 1/3 cup butter, melted
- 1 teaspoon cinnamon
- 1 cup coconut flour
- 1 teaspoon vanilla
- 3 tablespoons avocado oil
- 1/3 cup hazelnuts, chopped
- 2 cups of water
- 1 ½ teaspoon baking powder
- Frosting:
- 1 cup Sour cream
- 1 ½ cups Swerve, powdered
- ½ cup cream cheese
- 1/4 cup butter, softened

Nutritional Information

359 Calories
38.2g Fat
7g Carbs
14.3g Protein
4.1g Sugars

Directions

Add 2 cups of water and a metal rack to the Instant Pot. Lightly grease the cake pan with the melted butter.

In a large bowl mix the coconut flour, baking powder, cinnamon, and vanilla. Combine.

Then, in another bowl add the eggs, Swerve, carrots, and avocado oil. Mix well with an electric mixture.

Gradually stir in the dried mixture to the egg mixture.

Fold in the chopped hazelnuts. Pour the batter into the prepared cake pan. Cover the pan with a paper towel. Top with a piece of aluminum foil making a foil sling and lower the pan onto the rack.

Secure the lid. Choose "Manual" mode and Low pressure; cook for 32 minutes. When cooking is complete, use a natural pressure release and carefully remove the lid.

Meanwhile, in a bowl combine the cream cheese, Swerve, sour cream, and butter. Frost the cake and serve. Enjoy!

Summer Strawberry Yogurt

Ingredients

- 3 teaspoons probiotic yogurt starter
- 1 ½ cup fresh strawberries, sliced
- 1 teaspoon stevia powder
- 2 quarts raw milk

Nutritional Information

128 Calories
7.6g Fat
3.8g Carbs
8.9g Protein
4g Sugars

Directions

Add the raw milk to the Instant Pot.

Secure the lid. Choose the "Yogurt" mode. Press the "Adjust" button until you see the word "Boil". Turn off the Instant Pot.

Use a food thermometer to read the temperature; 110 degrees is good and then stir in the probiotic starter.

Press the "Yogurt" button again and then, press the "Adjust" button to reach 24 hours.

Place in your refrigerator for a few hours. Serve with fresh strawberries and stevia. Bon appétit!

Blueberry Mini Cheesecakes

Ingredients

- 1/2 cup almond flour
- 1/2 cup coconut flour
- 2 teaspoons baking powder
- ½ teaspoon salt
- ½ teaspoon grated nutmeg
- 1/2 teaspoon ground cinnamon
- 1/3 cup butter, melted
- 1/2 cup Swerve
- 2 eggs, beaten
- 1/2 cup plain yogurt
- ½ cup fresh blueberries
- 1/2 teaspoon vanilla
- 2 cups of water

Nutritional Information

171 Calories
14.1g Fat
3.9g Carbs
6.9g Protein
4g Sugars

Directions

Add 2 cups of water and a metal rack to your Instant Pot.

In a large bowl combine the almond flour, coconut flour, baking powder, salt, grated nutmeg, cinnamon, eggs, Swerve, vanilla, fresh blueberries, and yogurt.

Divide the batter between lightly greased ramekins. Cover with a piece of foil and place the ramekins on the rack.

Secure the lid. Choose "Manual" mode and High pressure; cook for 22 minutes. When cooking is complete, use a natural pressure release and carefully remove the lid.

Top with whipped cream and serve. Bon appetite!

Yummy Keto Flan

(Ready in about 20 minutes | Servings 5)

Ingredients

- 5 large eggs
- 1 cup Swerve
- 1 cup heavy cream
- 1/2 cup water
- ½ teaspoon salt
- 1/4 teaspoon ground cinnamon
- 1 teaspoon vanilla extract

Nutritional Information

140 Calories
13.4g Fat
1.3g Carbs
4.6g Protein
0.8g Sugars

Directions

Add 2 cups of water and a metal rack to your Instant Pot.

In a large bowl combine eggs and Swerve. Stir in salt, vanilla, water, cinnamon, and double cream.

Pour mixture into a baking dish and lower the dish onto the rack.

Secure the lid. Choose "Manual" mode and High pressure; cook for 11 minutes. When cooking is complete, use a natural pressure release and carefully remove the lid.

Leave to cool and serve. Enjoy!

Made in the USA
Monee, IL
03 June 2020